I Feel Heard:

How to Speak the Language of Emotions, Validate, and Truly Listen

By Patrick King

Social Interaction and Conversation Coach at
www.PatrickKingConsulting.com

Table of Contents

[INTRODUCTION](#) 7

[CHAPTER 1: UNDERSTANDING EMOTIONAL VALIDATION](#) 11

WHAT DO WE DO WHEN WE VALIDATE? 12
NORMALIZATION 19
PRACTICING NON-JUDGMENT 26
SIX LEVELS OF VALIDATION 33
IMAGO DIALOGUE SCRIPT 40

[CHAPTER 2: SPEAKING THE LANGUAGE OF EMOTION](#) 53

EMOTIONAL ACKNOWLEDGEMENT 54
AFFECT LABELLING FOR EMOTIONAL REGULATION 61
HELPING OTHERS IDENTIFY THEIR EMOTIONAL TRIGGERS 68
USING COMPLIMENTS 75

CHAPTER 3: BECOME A MASTER OF EMPATHETIC LISTENING — 81

WHEN WE LISTEN, WE VALIDATE	82
THE ART OF HOLDING SPACE	90
THE POWER OF SILENCE	97
LISTENING FOR EMOTIONAL METAPHORS	104
ACTIVE CONSTRUCTIVE RESPONDING	111

CHAPTER 4: WHAT NOT TO DO — 121

EMOTIONALLY INVALIDATING RESPONSES	122
AVOID GIVING UNWANTED ADVICE	129
FIGHTING TOXIC POSITIVITY	136
SELF-DISCLOSURE	143

CHAPTER 5: VALIDATION IN THE FACE OF CONFLICT — 151

WHEN IS VALIDATION NOT THE BEST APPROACH?	152
DO NOT VALIDATE NARCISSISTIC PEOPLE	160
VALIDATION DURING DISAGREEMENTS	166
DON'T GASLIGHT!	173
THE RESPONSIBILITY TO SELF-VALIDATE	181

Introduction

The modern world is a noisy place. With more than 8 billion of us as of 2024, it can feel like there are a lot of voices out there, each one desperate to be heard. Everyone wants to feel like they matter, and for the things they say to be heard and taken seriously. Few people are as interested in learning how to do the reverse, that is, how to *really listen to others.*

If you've picked up this book, then you are likely already convinced of the magic of learning to truly listen to people, to empathize with them, and to help them feel deeply understood and accepted. While our first impulse in communication is often to make sure that people understand *us*, the truth is that one of the best ways to improve relationships is to reverse this tendency, and get curious about other people, instead.

By being curious about others, you can learn:

- to understand exactly what emotional validation is (and isn't), and why people crave it so much.
- how to use the language of emotion to quickly reach people on a deep and sincere level.
- how to really listen (hint: so-called "active listening" is just the beginning).
- how to navigate emotionally difficult conversations, whether that's with loved ones, strangers, or colleagues.

The great thing is that these kinds of skills are available to anyone willing to learn.

Learning to emotionally validate someone just may be the quickest, easiest, and most enjoyable way to:

- Build greater intimacy and closeness
- Support and help others in ways that matter
- Create more authentic and resilient connections
- Smooth over conflict
- Make it more likely that *your* emotional needs will be met in turn.

In the chapters that follow we'll cover all of these, as well as some oft neglected ground, namely, what to do in situations where validation is actually the *wrong* response, and what to do about things like narcissism and gaslighting. Whatever your motivations and your current communication skills, rest assured that with a little willingness to put these principles into practice, you will soon be the kind of person that people trust, open up to, and love talking to. Let's dive in!

Chapter 1: Understanding Emotional Validation

Has anybody ever spoken to you in a way that made you feel completely worthless and unimportant?

Has anybody ever said or done something that made it seem like your thoughts, feelings, perceptions, or desires simply weren't legitimate or didn't matter?

Chances are, when that happened it made you feel misunderstood, disrespected, or maybe even a little crazy. What you felt was *invalidated*. This feeling you experienced is exactly what we're trying to avoid creating in others as we learn to respect, acknowledge, and accept their emotional realities.

In this first chapter we're going to get clear on exactly what we mean by the word validation, and what it means to *in*validate someone. We'll explore the importance of normalizing someone's emotions, and utilize some easy-to-follow steps, scripts, and outlines to help you begin your own practice of being a more emotionally validating communicator.

What do we do when we validate?

On a basic level, the word *valid* describes something sound, reasonable, rational, and logical. We use this word to talk about things that have a recognizable basis in fact, which we accept as more or less real. When we apply this word to someone's feelings and emotions, we are essentially saying, **"the way you feel is sound and reasonable, and I accept it as legitimate." Even more simply, emotional validation means we appraise someone's inner experience as something that *makes sense*.**

If we take the attitude that someone's emotional experience doesn't make sense, then we invalidate them. We may decide their perspective is weird, crazy, wrong, misguided, inferior, or just plain bad. We may judge, minimize, or even punish them for their emotions, and this can cause serious damage to relationships.

Research shows that invalidation experienced in childhood can lead to chronic emotional inhibition in adulthood (Krause et. al., 2003). Invalidation can damage a person's self-worth, disrupt their ability to emotionally regulate, trigger anxiety and depression, and lead to conflict, misunderstanding, and alienation. It doesn't require any special insight to see that emotional validation is a vital communication skill and an essential ingredient for all kinds of relationships.

When we are able to say that someone's feelings and perceptions are valid, we ultimately communicate a deeper message: *they themselves* are valid. By recognizing that their experience is legitimate, makes sense, and has a place in the world, we simultaneously communicate that they are worthy of being seen, heard, and acknowledged respectfully.

It would be wrong to assume that this skill comes automatically to most people. In fact, it usually requires deliberate practice to recognize that someone else's emotions are valid and to act accordingly. A reoccuring theme throughout this book is how accidental invalidation is our cultural norm, and that it takes a lot of mindfulness and humility to validate perspectives that are not our own.

A caveat: "valid" is not the same as "true"

Some of us stumble in the validation process because we think, "But how can I validate *that*? It's plain wrong!"

However, **validation is not the same as agreement**. We don't have to feel the same way that they feel in order to validate their feelings. Validating someone's emotion doesn't require us to invalidate our own, nor does it require us to invite poor treatment. When we validate an emotion, we are not saying that it is somehow "true" or that we endorse it in any way. All we are doing is recognizing that the person feels the way they feel, and that's OK. That's all.

A very simple example will illustrate the difference between validation and approval/agreement. Imagine a much-loved friend complains to you that they feel fat. The actual objective truth? They are a normal body weight and are not fat in the slightest. If you were to respond, "You're not fat!" you would be making a true claim that was nevertheless invalidating. It may even feel like this is a helpful and supportive statement, particularly since it's factually correct. But in reality, all you're doing is arguing against your friend's sincere experience. You are telling them, "The way you feel is not reasonable. It doesn't make sense. You don't make sense."

If you were to respond by saying, "I'm sorry. I know you often feel insecure about your appearance. Wanna talk about it?" instead, then you are practicing real emotional validation. You are not evaluating the truth of your friend's statement (which is not something they need you to do) nor are you agreeing with them that they are fat. Rather, you are validating their feelings. You are communicating that how they feel matters.

How to validate someone's emotions

When we remind ourselves that emotional validation has nothing to do with facts, nor with what is right or wrong, we are free to **simply listen** to what someone is going through, and to accept and acknowledge it with kindness.

Here is a simple step-by-step process that outlines the basics of the emotional validation process.

Step 1: Pay attention

One of the first and perhaps best ways to demonstrate to someone that their experience matters to you is to *pay attention to it!* When we grant something our full attention, we are giving it the status of something that is important enough to be acknowledged and recognized. You cannot make anyone feel seen or heard unless you first give them your undivided attention.

If someone is sharing something with you, or even if you're having an ordinary discussion, show respect for the other person and for your shared connection by being fully present, without distractions. Put your phone away, choose a place to talk that is quiet and conducive to conversation, physically turn to face them, and mentally focus your concentration on what they're saying.

Step 2: Practice allowing

Now that the stage is set and all distractions removed, it's time for the other person to open up and share. The biggest threat to them doing that fully is our own compulsion to jump in and add our interpretations, feelings, advice, reactions, questions, statements, or judgments.

Now, all of this can come from a good place, and we can find ourselves interrupting or simply because of a desire to help. Nevertheless, in order to properly validate their emotions, we need to keep quiet for a moment and just let them talk. This means active listening (which we will cover in more detail later) and resisting the temptation to judge or weigh in. Our goal during this step is to simply get out of the way, so that the other person can communicate their internal experience without us detracting from it in any way.

Step 3: Ask questions to understand

Only once the other person has finished fully expressing themselves are we in the position to step in with questions. Asking questions is a way to further validate, as it demonstrates our willingness to learn more and understand exactly what they're going through. An emotionally validating question shows others that we are listening, that we care about the details, and that on some level we are emotionally invested in those details.

By asking questions you are inviting the other person to explore and further unfold the experience they're trying to share with you, without rushing them or hurrying them along to a conclusion. By taking the time to confirm that we've heard correctly, we signal that we care about avoiding misunderstandings, and that accuracy matters. It's at this point that you can gently start putting names to their feelings (a technique called emotion labelling) so that they can start to summarize their feelings and pinpoint the deeper causes.

Be mindful, however, of the kind of questions you're asking. Your questions should seek to understand and validate, rather than to challenge or undermine. Ask open-ended, respectful questions that invite further exploration, rather than questions that subtly force them to justify or defend themselves. So, instead of asking "Why do you care about all this anyway?" you could ask, "What do you think it is about this situation that's bothering you so much?"

Step 4: Reflect, acknowledge, accept

Next, we validate. By mirroring their experience back to them with kindness and empathy, we show that it is not only safe to feel how they feel, but also safe to share openly with us what that's like for them. Though all the previous steps are validating to some degree, in this step we use directly validating statements, like:

- "I can see why you feel the way you do."
- "That make sense."
- "I can tell that this has really upset you."
- "That must have felt so XYZ for you."
- "I get you. It's understandable that you would think that."
- "I can totally see where you're coming from."

- "That sounds really difficult, thank you for telling me."
- "You have every right to feel that way!"

As you move through the steps above, your ultimate goal is to *be there* for the other person. Adjust your body language, facial expressions, eye contact, and attention so that they all communicate the same thing: **You matter. What you're feeling matters. I'm here to listen.**

Normalization

If you woke up one morning with a bizarre and truly frightening medical symptom, how would you feel?

Now, imagine you go to a doctor later that day who tells you, "Oh that? That happens to a lot of people. I see someone with this exact problem in my office at least once a day." Now how do you feel?

Normalization is closely connected to validation, and it's exactly what it sounds like: making something seem normal, regular, and completely expected. When we validate someone's emotions, we are making the claim that they make sense, and when we normalize them, we are saying that are expected and commonplace, i.e. there is nothing strange, abnormal, or out of the ordinary about them.

In cognitive behavior therapy (CBT) a therapist may try to make a client's experiences seem less overwhelming and distressing by pointing out that their experience is, essentially, normal. It may not be an easy, pleasant, or wanted experience, but knowing that it is fully within the realm of expected human experience can make it feel way more manageable. We feel less alone in our struggle.

When our feelings are normalized, we can remove any sense of shame or worry and recognize that our experience is not a sign of our unique struggle or failure, but rather a common experience we all encounter as human beings. What a relief! Even though this doesn't magically make problems disappear or challenges any easier, what it does create is a feeling of possibility and hope–if others have experienced it (and survived) then I can, too.

When normalizing, however, we still have to practice compassion and tact. To return to our example, if the doctor told you, "Oh that? That's nothing. Everybody suffers from that, don't think you're special! In fact, yours is a very mild case. Trust me, it could be so much worse…"

Naturally, when we normalize, we want to show that something is relatively common, expected, and even ordinary. We need to do this without suggesting that there is nothing unique about that person's experience, or that their concern is unwarranted. We need to be careful that we are not using normalization to *minimize* and indirectly invalidate.

We can avoid some of these pitfalls by reframing normalization: **it is not the issue itself that we are claiming is normal, but rather, we are reassuring someone that their response and feelings to it make sense given their beliefs**. So, for example, it may be that you have turned up to the doctor's office with a truly baffling health symptom that nobody has seen before. And yet, the doctor is being truthful when he says, "Look, everyone's body behaves a little strangely now and then. It makes sense that you're worried about it, that's a normal reaction that I see often." We *normalize the emotion*, not the situation.

Normalization is especially useful when a portion of a person's distress actually comes from secondary emotions that are triggered by primary emotions.

For example, someone might be having problems in their relationship, which are causing them to feel self-doubt (a primary emotion). Because they believe that nobody else experiences similar difficulties in relationships, they feel that their struggles are not normal. They feel shame and sadness (secondary emotions) because they imagine that they alone have made these specific errors, and that there is something wrong with them.

If we can listen and use normalization, we can reassure this person that their feelings of self-doubt are actually pretty normal. We can relieve some of the shame and sadness they feel. In the same way, we can help people stop feeling anxious about being depressed, or guilty about being angry, for example.

Plenty of people feel incredibly isolated in their distress because they wrongly believe that they are the only ones experiencing it. We tend to assume that there is something uniquely wrong with us when it comes to:

- Procrastination, lack of motivation, and laziness.
- Performance anxiety.
- Concerns about self-esteem and worth.
- Stress and overwhelm.
- Feeling lost in life or unsure of our next steps.

- Feeling disconnected from or annoyed by loved ones.

We may assume that we are the only ones to experience these challenges, and what's more, we may conclude that this is evidence that something is wrong with us as people. The truth, however, is that all of these things are human universals, and extremely common! When we normalize, we help people recognize this fact, which can be enormously reassuring.

In CBT, the therapist's goal is to help their client reappraise the world in more accurate and helpful ways. When we listen empathetically, validate emotions, and normalize a person's perceptions, we gently invite them to take on a worldview where they are not weird, abnormal, or bad.

In fact, a paper on the effects of CBT-style normalization used in treatment for those with schizophrenia found that it was extremely helpful in stabilizing mood, regulating threat appraisal, and reducing stigma (Dudley et.al., 2007, *Techniques in Cognitive Behavioural Therapy: Using Normalising in Schizophrenia*). The authors give an example of a normalizing and empathetic response to someone's neurotic and repetitive handwashing behavior: "So you believed you had poison on your hands and that you would be responsible for killing your children, well no wonder you felt anxious, and wanted to wash your hands."

Such a response does not agree nor disagree, and it's not about what is "right" or "wrong." There is no judgment at all, only a validation and normalization of the emotional response. "It makes sense that you'd desperately want to wash your hands if you thought they were contaminated and could hurt someone you love. Most people would feel the same. In fact, many people have these thoughts and feel the same way as you feel now."

Once we can validate and normalize someone's emotions, then they are free to move on and process those feelings, manage them, or set about solving the real-world problem that triggered them. Helping somebody normalize their experience doesn't mean we think it should remain the status quo. Quite the opposite: when we accept without resistance and shame, then we can help them move towards healthy problem solving and coping strategies.

Normalizing someone's experience is simple and takes very little time, but it does require a little mindfulness on our part. Here are a few things to keep in mind:

- Acknowledge that experiences and emotional reactions are common, without minimizing or invalidating them.
- Normalize the *emotion* and not the details of the event itself. For example, someone may have acted poorly in anger. You can normalize their angry feelings without condoning their behavior.
- Draw a connection between the situation, their appraisal, and their emotional reaction, showing that this connection is largely sound and sane. For example, "Given that you were already stressed and confused, it makes sense that you lashed out that way. It's not uncommon for people with a history of trauma to respond in that way."
- Keep the conversation going. While their experience may not be strictly unique in the world, it's unique to them. Just because it's a common experience doesn't mean you can't ask for more details, or invite them to talk more about how they felt. We've all felt sad in life, for example, but that doesn't mean that anyone's sadness is insignificant!

Practicing non-judgment

Are you a judgmental person?

Most people would fervently deny it. After all, aren't you reading a book on how to be more validating and compassionate?

Unfortunately, the everyday judgments that most of us are guilty of are subtle, automatic, and often well-meaning. In other words, **we can be judgmental without realizing it, or worse, we can mistakenly think that our judgment is necessary or helpful.**

Let's consider some common manifestations of judgment:

- Criticizing people (i.e., telling them that they're doing something wrong)
- Shaming (i.e. telling them that *they themselves* are wrong)
- Deciding that someone is inferior or unworthy
- Punishing someone's behavior or feelings
- Prejudice, bias, and making assumptions about who someone is
- Forcing our own interpretations onto someone else's behavior
- Automatically assuming that our perspective is the right one

- Using feedback to attack and undermine someone

It's pretty obvious that the above behaviors are invalidating and bound to damage relationships. Being judgmental can seriously impair our communication skills, break trust, and lead to all sorts of tensions and hostilities. In reality, few people are ever judgmental in such blatant, obvious ways. Instead, they may be judgmental in more subtle, and arguably more damaging, ways.

Consider an example: someone is taking a long time to reply to a text message. You think, "He's so rude. He's a jerk who thinks everyone else is beneath him."

Now, pause for a moment. Notice how this response is not actually an observation of the facts. Here, all that is factually known is that he has not replied to a text message. The rest? Just an interpretation. A harsh one, at that.

Our most damaging forms of judgment often come wrapped up in interpretations about other people's behaviors. We are quick to spin narratives about who they are and what their lives mean. We make assumptions about their intentions, and sometimes even assume we have unique insight into their deeper motivations. In other words, our judgment can take the form of deciding, all on our own, what someone else's life means.

In the above example, we have chosen one particular story to explain the behavior; he is rude and thinks he's better than other people. But there are other possible explanations. He could be genuinely busy. He could have ADHD and have problems with organization. He could have merely forgotten. He could be ignoring the text because it makes him uncomfortable. He could even be failing to respond because he perceives the text as an impossible demand, and is avoiding it because it makes him feel worse than others, not better...

So, which is the right interpretation?

The answer is: *none of them*. In order to truly listen, validate, and show genuine compassion for people, we need to hold off on making any judgments or interpretations at all.

When we listen, we are not called to make a decision about whether we agree with what we're hearing or not. We do not listen in order to gather up facts and decide whether they're legitimate or not, or to pick which side we agree with. We are not validating people's emotions on the basis of our agreement with them.

To put it simply, **judgmental interpretations hinder our empathetic listening and our ability to truly validate someone.**

But what if the guy really *is* a jerk?

There is nothing wrong with making appraisals and estimations, being discerning, or having your own boundaries and opinions. However, it's important that that all comes *after* we've properly heard and seen the person in front of us, not before. Otherwise, communication is never really possible–we will be too busy telling our own narrative to hear theirs, and vice versa. It's not difficult to see how judgment on both sides of a dialogue can quickly lead to conflict and communication breakdown.

The most important thing to bear in mind is that **judgment is completely unnecessary for emotionally validating communication.** We can listen to someone's emotional experience, enter into their world and consider their perspective, all without it threatening our own, or costing us anything. We can listen without ever making value judgments about their experience, and we can support them even while we might hold different opinions, goals, and values.

In fact, dropping the tendency to judge, interpret, or appraise what people are telling us only brings benefits: more open and honest dialogue, more trust and intimacy, and the relief of knowing that we are never really required to solve everyone's problems or come up with a clever explanation for what they're going through. Our only job, really, is to listen with kindness.

Avoid "positive judgment" too

We unwittingly invalidate people when we force our own interpretations onto their lives, even if those interpretations are "positive." We will explore toxic positivity in a later chapter, but for now it's worth considering the judgmental interpretations we may default to when we sincerely want to help.

Consider this example. A friend has signed up to do a course, but is now in over her head and seriously thinking about quitting. She's exhausted, she's overwhelmed, and she's wondering why she ever signed up in the first place. "I'm just not sure this is right for me. I'm not sure I can do it." she says. Hearing this, and wanting to be as kind and helpful as possible, you immediately jump in and say, "You *can* do it! You've got to have a little faith in yourself. You're amazing and you're going to get through this, I know you will."

Even though you have responded with the very best of intentions, you've actually invalidated your friend's emotional reality, and furthermore, you've forced your own interpretation onto it. While her narrative was one of uncertainty and second-guessing the fit and appropriateness of the course, your response has framed the dilemma in terms of self-belief and confidence. This is a "positive judgment" that nevertheless may be experienced as invalidating.

When we come into a conversation with any form of prejudgment, we make it difficult for others to share how they actually feel. If people know that their words will be pressed through a pre-existing filter, it makes it harder for them to open up–even if that filter was set up out of kindness. Ultimately, it comes down to a lack of empathy. We all have the tendency to make snap judgments and assumptions, but we need to consistently remind ourselves that our perspective may not align with theirs.

Any time we encounter miscommunication, there is a good chance that misjudgment has happened somewhere earlier along the line. If we keep quiet, listen, and pay close attention, we may realize that the explanatory story we were quick to adopt was actually quite far off the mark!

Pause and check in with yourself

It's extremely easy to fall into pre-judgment of others, but with a little intentional practice, we can start to learn to open our minds, truly listen, and be willing to learn something from people who inhabit their own entirely unique inner worlds.

- Reflect regularly on your own biases and expectations.
- Be on guard for a tendency to "compete" in social interactions, for example jumping in to one-up others or immediately comparing their experience against yours.
- Notice if you have a tendency to elevate yourself or assume an attitude of one who has ultimate authority over what the right answer is. Pay close attention to any time you may be preaching, lecturing, explaining, or giving advice.
- Never assume that other people think or feel as you do, that they have the same values or goals, or that they interpret things in the same way. In fact, assume nothing until you're told otherwise!
- Let go of any desire to decide what your opinion is about someone else's situation. We can always choose not to react.

- When in doubt, stick to the facts. What do you know is definitively true? Let go of the rest and be willing to say, "I don't know."
- When reflecting someone's experience back to them, use neutral language, or repeat the words they themselves use, instead of introducing your own.
- Be honest about your own emotions about what others are sharing. In the above example, your own struggles with low self-esteem may have primed you to interpret your friend' story in the particular way you did.
- Deliberately choose to maintain a curious and open-minded attitude. Be willing to learn more and choose to encounter differences or uncertainties without seeing them as a threat.

In the example above, a more validating response may simply be, "You're not sure it's right for you? Oh man, that sounds tricky. Can you tell me more? Why do you worry the course may not be right for you?" With this, your friend feels seen, heard, and reassured– and she will probably want to open up to you more.

Six levels of validation

So, we know that validating and normalizing emotional responses can help us communicate empathetically, and that judgment can hinder that communication. We've also briefly touched on the benefits of reflecting, listening, and supporting others as they open up and share with us.

In this section, we will use the work of Dr. Marsha Linehan, the creator of Dialectical Behavior Therapy (DBT), to help us start pulling some of these threads together. According to Linehan, **there are six different degrees or levels of validation**, which increase in intensity.

Not every interaction is going to need 100% full-force empathy and validation, but sometimes we offer a level of support that is not sufficient for the task at hand. By examining the varying depths or degrees of validation, we can stay mindful and learn to **match our response to the situation** and the needs of the person we're talking to.

Level 1: Attention

As we've already seen, it all begins with paying complete, undivided attention to what you're being told. You can show that you're listening in both verbal and non-verbal ways:

- Nodding
- Asking clarifying questions
- Eye contact

- Adjusting your facial expression as appropriate
- Making supportive and acknowledging sounds (uh-huh, mmm)
- Using your body language to express interest and focus
- Matching your expression to theirs; for example, lowering your voice when their voice is lowered

Ask yourself: Am I listening fully?

Level 2: Empathetic reflection

The next level takes things a little further. Like a mirror, we offer back a picture of the image we're seeing, and we echo the sentiments we've heard. As we've seen, we can do this primarily by asking questions that clarify, ("So what happened next? She left?") summarize, ("It seems like all in all you were pretty confused.") and confirm our comprehension ("You never saw her again, is that right?").

By paraphrasing and reflecting back not only the words but the nonverbal parts of the story being shared, it's as though we hold up a mirror and ask, "I have a picture here, is this accurate?" By doing this we confirm that we've received the message loud and clear, and we convey respect and our genuine intention to understand.

Ask yourself: Am I accurately able to reflect the message being shared with me?

Level 3: Saying the unspoken part out loud

To go into an even deeper level of validation, we start to look beyond the verbal content of the message and consider the emotional, usually unarticulated portion of the message.

At this level, you are actively doing a lot more work than merely listening and reflecting. You are making educated guesses and inferences about what the person is really feeling – and this is largely unspoken. We will investigate this skill set in more detail in Chapter 3. For now, the goal is to (gently!) suggest possible labels for emotions that people may be feeling, which can help them process and better understand their own experience. These suggestions are best framed as questions, rather than foregone conclusions or, as we saw earlier, judgmental interpretations.

Try to help the person put a name to their feeling, or to summarize their words into a single word or expression. "It sounds like you're feeling pretty frustrated with it all right now, if I've understood you correctly" or "I wonder if you feel a little bit angry about the situation?" Asking thoughtful and meaningful follow-up questions shows that you're paying close attention, but on a deeper level.

Ask yourself: Am I able to ask meaningful follow-up questions to confirm what they're feeling? Can I accurately reflect the nonverbal aspects of the message being shared with me?

Level 4: Validating

Beyond being able to listen and reflect both verbal and nonverbal material, is the ability to offer validation, and place the story you're hearing in a broader context. Linehan suggests considering the person's own history or biology; for example, acknowledging that tiredness or illness explains and contextualizes feelings of despair or fatigue, or that a person's history or childhood may predispose them to certain reactions or patterns of behavior.

Doing this does not mean you're looking for excuses or justifications, but it does mean that you're helping the other person see that given other factors, their response makes sense and is reasonable and normal. Connecting things in this way can help people feel less alone, more understood, and more justified in their experience. Even more broadly speaking, are there cultural, social, economic, or generational factors that could help account for and explain their emotional experience?

Ask yourself: Am I able to place the message I'm hearing in a broader context, and consider the bigger picture?

Level 5: Normalizing

As before, normalizing often goes alongside validating. However, Linehan considers normalizing to be at a rather deep level, meaning that it's not necessary or appropriate for every situation or relationship. We can say things like, "Anyone in your situation would feel exactly the same," or "we all have that experience sooner or later." However, we need to be cautious and avoid dismissing people's concerns or overlaying our own interpretive filter over their experience.

One thing to watch out for is normalizing genuinely unhealthy or abnormal behaviors. In the realm of human emotion, we can take the view of Roman playwright Terence Lucanus, who claimed, "Nothing human is alien to me." While all *emotions* may be normal, there are some *behaviors* that should not be encouraged, normalized, or excused.

When in doubt, chose to focus on the small "grain of truth" that is present in everyone's experience and perception, and remind yourself to normalize and validate the feeling, without making judgments about any resulting behaviors.

Ask yourself: Am I able to normalize the emotion I'm hearing, whether it's spoken or unspoken?

Level 6: Radical Genuineness

The highest level of empathetic listening and validation is, according to Linehan, about complete authenticity and respect on your part. You are not just receiving and accurately processing a message; you are also adopting a particular attitude towards the person sharing that information: an attitude of deep respect for them as a fellow human being, and seeing them as your equal.

This means neither elevating nor denigrating them, neither excusing them nor judging them. Instead, this level of validation is characterized by the genuineness of your own response to what you're hearing, and your willingness to bring a little bit of your own humanity into the picture. Here is your chance for appropriate self-disclosure, acknowledgement of your own limitations, and a more honest expression of your own feelings about the matter at hand.

Ask yourself: Am I being radically genuine with this person?

In real life, of course, things will not be so clearly delineated. The six levels described above, however, can help us understand that emotional validation falls on a spectrum. It's worth understanding where our communication should fall on that spectrum, given the circumstances.

For more casual or quick encounters that are largely superficial, you will seldom need to go beyond level 3 – merely paying kind attention, reflecting, and possibly offering some emotional labeling will be enough. Stay at these levels when you don't know the person very well, when the situation is not too serious, or when you're in a professional context. We can be emotionally validating even in our small talk, but it's wise to limit ourselves to attentive listening and avoid trying to be radically genuine with strangers at a bus stop!

The deeper levels are more appropriate for people we know very well or have a history with, for serious or emotionally challenging situations, and for close relationships, like within a family or marriage. Here, a little more is required of us if we hope to make others feel truly seen and heard.

Imago dialogue script

If you've read up to this point and thought, "That all sounds fine, but what do I actually *say* in the moment?" then you're in luck, this next section is for you! Though we've outlined some general principles for validating and normalizing someone's emotions, without judgment, at some point we need to find a way to bring all this into real life.

Imago Dialogue is one approach that can help us get really specific about what to say and do in emotional conversations–particularly in conflicts and arguments. This theory and approach was originally developed by Harville Hendrix, PhD, and Helen LaKelly Hunt, PhD. It contains three key steps for rebuilding connection. In fact, you'll recognize these steps as they are the very same principles we've covered already.

The Imago Relationship Theory was specifically created for couples, and the goal is to transform conflict into opportunities for growth, understanding and connection. Using a structured "script," the Sender (the one who speaks) and the Receiver (the one who listens) move through a sequence that encourages active listening, emotional validation, and respectful requests. We can use this theory to help us become better listeners, and use conversations to create more trust, understanding, and closeness.

There are a few things to note about this approach before we take a closer look, however. The three-step process may seem a little too obvious and straightforward, and in a way, it is. The real insight comes with *applying* it in real life. When we're in the middle of a difficult conversation or emotions are running high, it's extremely easy to forget ourselves. The simplicity of the Imago script is precisely what keeps us on track.

Another point is that the language encouraged here can feel a little, well, stilted. Though there is plenty of research to support the theory's effectiveness, you may find the "therapy speak" a little unnatural or awkward to use–at first. What's important is that you understand the principles and can learn to apply them; over time, the approach will become second nature and not quite as artificial as it might first seem.

The process unfolds in three steps: Mirroring, Validation, and Empathy. As we've already seen, there is power in dropping judgment, and **listening in order to understand and connect, rather than listening in order to respond (or even defend).** Starting from a position of mutual respect and equality, the Sender and the Receiver draw closer together, understand one another better, and move on from misunderstandings.

We'll look at each step below, but also give literal phrases and sentences that you can use in your own life. Memorizing a script verbatim is not recommended, since it may prevent you from being present in the moment and may come across as insincere. That said, these phrases and words can be used as a temporary crutch as you build your confidence and gradually find ways to make them your own.

Preparation

Before the dialogue begins, it has to be arranged properly, rather than randomly sprung on people unawares. This gives everyone time to get mentally ready and ensures that there is time, space, and privacy available for a genuine connection to take place. Difficult or emotional conversations are a little like airplane flights–takeoff and landing are the most important parts!

Either Sender or Receiver can initiate a dialogue, but for obvious reasons it's usually the Sender who prompts things by saying things like:

- "I'd like to have a conversation about XYZ, can we talk?"
- "Is now a good time?"
- "When would you prefer to have a dialogue with me? Can we make a plan to talk later?"
- "I'm feeling bothered/unsure/unconnected/confused about XYZ and need to

talk/share/confirm/ask about something."

Step 1: Mirror

Once both parties have agreed to connect and are on the same page, the conversation begins with the Sender speaking first. They share their feelings and experiences using factual language and "I" statements where appropriate. Though they have "the floor," their responsibility is to speak without judgment, shame, or blame. So, they would say "I feel rejected." instead of "You've rejected me!"

They take care to express their feelings accurately, and claim them as their own, rather than sneaking in interpretations or judgments. That means saying, "I feel so sad" instead of, say, "Your unresolved mother issues are triggering me, and I don't know why you can't see that the only way forward is a break." (There are too many assumptions to count!)

Then, the Receiver repeats everything they've heard, without including a scrap of their own commentary, interpretation, analysis, or critique. The goal is just to confirm the message that was sent has been received intact and in full.

Say:

- "If I am understanding you correctly, I think you're saying…"
- "So what you're saying is…"
- "OK, I heard you say that XYZ, and you've also mentioned ABC."
- "Have I got all of that? Have I heard you?"
- "Let me see if I've got you…"

That's the very first step. *Nothing* else comes before it. If someone says, "I'm really disappointed with this gift you got me" then an appropriate Imago step 1 response would be: "So you're saying that you're disappointed with the gift I got you." While you don't want to literally mimic them like a parrot, do try to make minimal changes in your paraphrasing.

The Sender continues to speak and send their message, with the Receiver mirroring it, until the message is sent in full. Importantly, the Receiver is not just saying the right words in order to placate the Sender or to check a box; they are genuinely taking the time to gain a full and accurate understanding of the other person's emotional reality before moving on. Again, you don't have to agree with or like what is being said, but you can hear and respect it. That's harder than it sounds!

Step 2: Validate

When the Sender indicates that they are finished, the Receiver then validates that message. Take care that the validation happens *after* the mirroring–you cannot validate what you haven't confirmed you understand. As before, validate by affirming that the message sent by the Sender makes sense and is reasonable. If it doesn't make sense? The Receiver asks clarifying questions until it does.

This step avoids conflict and misunderstanding because, remember, we are validating emotions–not arguing about facts.

Say:

- "That makes sense to me because…"
- "I can see what you mean with this…"
- "That sounds fair and reasonable to me."

In our example, the Receiver might ask a few more clarifying questions about why the Sender feels disappointed with the gift.

Say:

- "OK, I understand when you say XYZ, but can you explain what you mean by ABC?"
- "That part makes sense to me, but can you help me understand why you say XYZ?"

Eventually, when the Sender is finished expressing themselves, the Receiver can say, "Hm, I get that. It makes sense that you would feel disappointed if you thought that I hadn't put any effort in. I can see that it's important to you that gifts are meaningful and thoughtful."

Step 3: Empathize

The Empathize step is a little like Dr. Linehan's "saying the unspoken part out loud." The Receiver tries to guess (without judgment) what the Sender is feeling based on what they've shared. Again, this is not the place to add in sneaky judgments or interpretations. In fact, feelings are often best described by single words: sad, lonely, angry, confused, etc.

Of course, the Sender may have already said directly what they are feeling, in which case the Receiver then reflects and confirms these feelings, with as little distortion as possible.

Say:

- "It seems like you're feeling XYZ… Is that how you are feeling now?"
- "I would guess that you're feeling ABC about all this… am I on the right track?"
- "Are you feeling XYZ right now?"

So, for example, the Receiver might say, "I imagine you feel unseen or unappreciated when you receive a gift that seems thoughtless. Is that how you're feeling right now?"

The Sender might agree, disagree, or suggest adjustments. "Yes, I feel unseen, but it's more like I'm worried that you don't really know me at all, and that makes me feel scared and alone."

Then the Receiver would say, "Ah, I think I understand better. You're also feeling scared and worried."

So, what happens after the three steps have been completed? According to Hendrix and Hunt, the process repeats again, but this time with the roles of Sender and Receiver reversed. Depending on the nature of the conflict, the process may require several switches back and forth. Though this may seem cumbersome, when compared to the endless circles some couples can go around in (sometimes for years!), the technique may actually save time and smooth over conflicts quicker.

Now, the Imago method was created specifically for couples, and its intended use is during conflict and misunderstanding–not everyday interactions. However, we can adapt the main insights from this theory to give our own communication skills a real edge. There's a lot we can take from Hendrix and Hunt's theory that is applicable to all sorts of situations and relationships, namely:

It is never up to us to judge whether we really understand someone and have heard them or not–that's for *them* to determine! The only way we can be sure we've truly understood is to confirm it with the only person who knows, i.e. the Sender. If there is a mismatch between our version of their life and theirs, then we are likely the mistaken ones. Try to remember that it's not up to you to guess and assume. Want to know how someone feels? *Ask them*. Then really listen to what you're told.

Prioritize understanding, connection, and reception of someone's complete message before you jump in to respond or share your own message–no matter how tempting it may be to skip ahead!

Finally, language matters. Be aware of how your own choice of words can allow interpretation, judgment, blame, assumptions, and expectations to creep in. The more emotionally difficult a situation, the more careful you need to be. Stick to expressions that are factual and feelings-based, i.e. "nonviolent communication."

Summary

- Emotional validation is an essential part of healthy communication in relationships of every kind. When we validate someone's emotions, we confirm that the way that they feel is sound, reasonable, legitimate, and makes sense. Ultimately, this communicates that they-as people-are valid, too.
- Validation does not mean we agree with, condone, or even understand another person's feelings, only that we recognize that they feel as they feel.
- There are many steps to emotional validation, including: paying attention, allowing people to speak while offering empathetic reflection, asking questions to invite sharing, emotion labeling to "speak the unspoken part out loud", validating either nonverbally or with validating statements, normalizing, and, if appropriate, demonstrating radical genuineness.
- We should normalize and validate feelings, not behaviors or events.
- According to Dr. Marsha Linehan, emotional validation falls on a scale of increasing intensity and should be

matched to the needs of the occasion and relationship.
- The imago dialogue is a structured way to mirror, validate, and empathize with people. Though designed for couples navigating conflicts, it can teach us important principles about communicating more empathetically in any relationship.
- These principles include first fully allowing a person to share their message before going in with our own interpretations, judgments, or feelings.

Chapter 2: Speaking the Language of Emotion

Emotional invalidation is sadly an epidemic in our world. Most of us are in the habit of ignoring or downplaying other peoples' emotional realities, and have likely been on the receiving end of this kind of treatment ourselves. *We* are the ones who most frequently invalidate our own emotions. In other words, **it's a cultural norm to elevate and prioritize the rational, the mental, and the factual, and disregard the personal, the emotional, and the subjective**.

Learning to become more empathetic communicators requires that we know how to shift out of the default "objective" mindset and pay closer attention to the world of emotions. Most of us receive no formal training in this area and can't honestly say we are surrounded by positive role models. This means that even if we have the best of intentions, we tend to not know how to make this switch.

This chapter is all about becoming more *emotionally literate* in general. That means not only learning to read and validate emotions in others, but also becoming more adept overall at "speaking the language of emotions," whether we're talking about our own or those of others. Let's take a closer look.

Emotional acknowledgement

Imagine that you have received really poor service from a company you've been loyal to for years and have phoned customer service to make a complaint. It's not a question of money; rather, you're feeling angry and insulted that the company was inconsiderate in their treatment of you, and you now have a burning sense of injustice about the situation.

On the phone, however, you are met with a robotic, officious voice that appears to be reading from a script. You keep making requests for help, and you keep trying to make your point, but at every turn the customer service representative is obstructive and maddeningly polite. After an enraging conversation, they agree to issue you a refund and before you know it, the call is terminated.

You are immediately emailed a request to rate the service you've received. "Have we resolved your issue?" the email asks. You ponder this for a moment. The operator was polite, efficient, and issued you a full refund in record time. But then why do you still feel so mad?

One potential explanation: your feelings have been completely (and professionally!) invalidated. Granted, feelings generally don't have a place in the commercial world, but you gradually realize the real source of your lingering anger: the person on the other side of the line *did not acknowledge your anger*. They did not recognize that you felt wronged, that you felt that you were treated unfairly, and that you were, quite rightly, upset. In fact, the interaction proceeded as though your feelings on the matter were entirely irrelevant.

Emotional acknowledgement is recognizing someone's emotional state, and that usually means verbally expressing that you have noticed it, you are aware of it, and that it has been registered as a real and valid part of the social interaction. If you've ever experienced the lack of emotional acknowledgment as described above, you'll know how bad it feels. Incidentally, this is a big part of why so many apologies fail to make people feel better!

We briefly touched on emotion labeling earlier, and this is what emotional acknowledgment essentially amounts to. It's a simple thing, but it has profound significance.

Let's say you notice a nonverbal cue in someone else; for example, a slight frown or a happy tone of voice. You then acknowledge and reflect this by saying, "You seem unsure about that." or "You sound so happy!" This allows you to validate, reflect, and acknowledge that person's emotional reality, all in a statement that takes a mere moment to make.

Researcher Alison Yu became interested in this phenomenon while speaking to pediatric nurses working at a hospital in Stanford. The nurses explained that when they *verbally acknowledged* the fears and anxieties the children were experiencing, those children trusted them more, and they were able to do their jobs more effectively.

Teaming up with two other Harvard Business School professors, Yu conducted a series of studies to examine the impact of emotional acknowledgement in the workplace. They published their findings in *Science Direct* (Yu et. al., 2021) and the results were clear: **Emotional validation has positive benefits for all involved**.

But why should giving a name to someone else's emotion create trust? Doesn't the other person already know how they feel? The answer may lie in what Yu and fellow researchers describe as the *cost of emotional engagement in social situations*. They claim,

> *"We draw upon Costly Signaling Theory to posit how emotional acknowledgment influences interpersonal trust. We hypothesize that emotional acknowledgment acts as a costly signal of the perceiver's willingness to expend personal resources to meet the needs of the expresser. Across six studies, we found convergent evidence that emotional acknowledgment led to greater perceptions of costliness, and in turn, to higher evaluations of trust. These effects were stronger for negative than positive emotions because acknowledging negative emotions involved a greater perceived cost."*

To put this in simple terms, acknowledging someone else's emotions incurs a small cost. If we demonstrate that we are willing to take on that cost, and do that work, so to speak, we are making an attempt to invest in the other person, and to commit in a real way to the connection we share. In a very basic sense, this signals that we care. People find it easier to trust us.

We can take this further. Why should we feel reassured by someone else making an attempt to "expend personal resources" on our behalf? That may be because we ourselves have taken a risk in expressing our emotions in the first place. To show how we feel incurs a cost too, because it makes us slightly vulnerable, and exposes us to... well, the invalidation of others!

When someone sees, acknowledges, and *reciprocates* the risk you've taken, you trust them more. If you read back through the example we began with, you may now see how the unspoken unwillingness of the customer service representative to expend even the tiniest amount of emotional energy was actually the real cause of the bad feeling that the hypothetical you was left with.

The Costly Signal Theory actually originated in the 70s with evolutionary biologist Amotz Zahavi. According to Zahavi, even very small acts of such emotional willingness can be powerful because they are an "honest signal" of a person's desire for genuine connection. This may explain why Yu and colleagues found that emotional acknowledgement didn't even have to be accurate to have this positive effect:

> *"Moreover, inaccurate acknowledgment fostered greater trust than not acknowledging when positive emotions were mislabeled as negative, but not when negative emotions were mislabeled as positive."*

What matters, ultimately, is that someone has expended time and energy trying to connect with us.

How can we put this information to use in our own lives? Yu suggests that relationships improve when people consciously signal their concern for others' emotional state, and a willingness to put "skin in the game," so to speak.

She explains, "A leader could very easily see someone in distress and choose to ignore it. But only a leader who truly is benevolent and cares about employees would risk getting involved by voluntarily acknowledging the distressed employee. Thus, employees might take this as a signal that this leader is someone who can be trusted with their well-being."

If you want to inspire trust, get people to open up and create genuine connections, you *cannot* stand off to the side, unwilling to get emotionally involved–especially when people have taken the risk of expressing negative emotions. Fail to acknowledge people's emotions and you may be perceived as aloof, uninterested, or untrustworthy.

Don't think that you need to become everyone's tireless therapist, however; trust and a feeling of goodwill can be created by simple emotional labelling. **Even incorrectly labelling an emotion is better than ignoring it entirely**. After all, as we saw with the Imago script above, when you frame an acknowledgement or observation as a question, you can invite people to correct you, which opens a dialogue.

"Have I got that right?" signals that yes, you may not fully understand where they're coming from… but you're there and you're willing to find out. If you're feeling unsure or as though you don't want to say the wrong thing, that's OK–what matters is that you're acknowledging that an emotion is happening at all. 100% accuracy is not required.

Gently shift your attention from events and situations and show concern for the people involved. It is validating to say, "That seems like a difficult situation," but it is far more validating to say, "You seem a bit overwhelmed. How are you feeling about it all?" Yu further says, "There's just something special and unique about emotions. They are really core to a person's inner experience and sense of self. So when we acknowledge emotions, we humanize and validate the person being acknowledged."

Emotional acknowledgment, at the end of the day, isn't very "costly" at all.

1. Notice nonverbal cues that suggest emotion, like facial expressions, voice quality, or body language.
2. Acknowledge them. Frame your observation gently, possibly as a question. Say, "you seem…" or "it looks like…" and offer a feeling word.
3. Stay open. Your label is not the end of the discussion, but the beginning. Don't be afraid to ask if your perception is correct–what's important is that you signal that you care.

Affect labelling for emotional regulation

According to Yu's research, it would seem that the "active ingredient" in emotional acknowledgment is not a sophisticated vocabulary, mind-reading powers, or comprehensive psychiatric knowledge. **What really matters is effort, care, and demonstrated intention to connect**. That said, there is some *additional* value, naturally, in knowing the precise words for different emotions. **Affect labeling, i.e., putting words to vague emotions and feelings, is a way to**

manage, moderate, and regulate our emotions and the emotions of others.

Imagine that, after you have your annoying phone call with the customer service representative, you later have a chat with your partner about the incident. You're still riled up and immediately start complaining. Your partner listens patiently, then says this: "It almost sounds like you feel a little embarrassed by the whole thing."

This gives you pause, and you ponder this for a moment. They're right! Now that they mention it, that's *exactly* what you're feeling. You realize that it's as though, when they failed to acknowledge and validate your anger, you began to feel like there might be something shameful or inappropriate about losing your temper on the phone. You were angry, but their failure to react to that anger made you feel judged for being unreasonable. The result was a strange pang of humiliation.

Your partner has not only listened and validated your emotion, but they've done something more–they've helped you better understand what you're actually feeling. The ability to do this comes down to simply knowing the right word to assign to that particular sensation: embarrassment.

When someone is inside their emotion, that feeling is flooding their entire world and coloring their perception, so they may not know what they're feeling–only that they're feeling it. Incidentally, if you've ever wondered why the question, "How does that make you feel?" can seem so annoying, this may explain it. People in the midst of a strong emotion may *really not know*, and the demand to suddenly switch emotional gears can feel utterly impossible.

An alternative is to offer your own perspective and perception. **Affect labeling puts a word to someone's experience and helps them temporarily step outside of it.** This creates psychological distance, dials down the emotional intensity, and makes things seem much more manageable. You essentially help that person to self-validate, i.e. to give reassurances that they make sense to themselves!

Emotional regulation requires awareness– yours!

While it may seem obvious to some, it's a fact worth spelling out: **We cannot regulate our emotions if we don't know that we're having emotions, or what our emotions actually are.** Affect labeling is the first step to getting a handle on our experiences, and to do that we need to be aware enough of what is happening. If we wish to become more compassionate listeners and more emotionally validating friends and family members, then we need to learn to help people with this process.

This requires that we ourselves possess a basic level of emotional intelligence and self-awareness, since we can't understand signs and cues in others if we can't even recognize them in ourselves. It also requires that we have a fully stocked inventory of vocabulary to describe emotions, and that we be mature enough to face emotions that can be difficult.

If we don't know ourselves well, we risk projecting our own feelings onto others and forcing our own interpretations on them. If we don't have a full emotional vocabulary, we risk understanding people but being unable to meaningfully express it... which amounts to the same as not understanding them. We may become like those people who impotently say, "I know how you feel" knowing it provides little comfort.

If we hope to inspire and enable others to build more self-awareness, we need to be building our own self-awareness, too. In fact, one study found that being able to monitor and precisely describe emotions was a protective factor against depression and enabled people to cope better.

Dr. Lisa Starr, research lead, explains that "Adolescents who use more granular terms such as 'I feel annoyed,' or 'I feel frustrated,' or 'I feel ashamed'–instead of simply saying 'I feel bad'–are better protected against developing increased depressive symptoms after experiencing a stressful life event" (Starr et. al., 2020).

What Starr is describing in Negative Emotion Differentiation (NED) which is the ability to discern between different shades of emotion. It takes honesty, maturity, and big heaps of self-compassion.

"Our data suggests that if you are able to increase people's NED then you should be able to buffer them against stressful experiences and the depressogenic effect of stress."

In other words, **if you can name it, you can tame it**. Emotions contain useful data that, if we have enough presence of mind, can be used to improve our lives. This applies to us but also to the people around us. Emotion labelling creates helpful psychological distance, whether it's initiated by us or by someone else who is trying to help.

If we can encourage a person to understand what they're feeling, they have a better idea of how that experience will unfold, and how to regulate themselves in the moment. If there's a word for how they feel, this may automatically have a normalizing and validating effect–if other people have even invented a term for this sensation, then how bad can it be? Knowing the words for things allows us to talk about what we're experiencing, so we can communicate better and ask for (the right) help.

By becoming more emotionally literate and helping others put finer and more accurate labels on their emotional experience, we bring more trust, honesty and intimacy into every conversation, whether it's a deep or superficial one. The better people are able to regulate emotionally, the lower the chances of conflict or misunderstanding– which is probably why the Imago script mentioned earlier emphasizes emotional labelling as part of active listening. It diffuses tension and prevents defensiveness, which is in everyone's interests.

We already know that a great way to label emotions is to make polite suggestions, observations, and guesses:

"You seem…"

"You sound…"

"It looks like…"

"I've noticed that…"

"I wonder if you feel…"

"I'm guessing that…"

"Do you think you're feeling…"

We can carry this further though and use labelling language in more targeted ways.

Way one: Incisive questioning

To be incisive means to be clear, focused, and accurately analytical. An incisive question is like a knife that helps you cut to the real heart of the matter (almost literally–the word comes from the Latin *incidere*, meaning cutting or penetrating). An incisive question is a thoughtful one that follows up meaningfully from what you already know. If someone says they feel awful, you could ask a question that invites them to refine this word a little.

"Awful… what do you think you really mean by that?"

"When you say awful, do you mean that you're feeling physically unwell, or is it more a feeling of emotional upset?"

"Oh, I get that. It makes sense you'd feel awful. What specifically is bothering you about all this?"

Use tact, thoughtfulness, and kindness as you guide someone to pinpoint the more "granular" description of how they're feeling.

Way two: Offer options

It's not always easy for someone to answer these questions. Sometimes it can help if you narrow the field of possibilities a little and ask them to choose between two options.

"When you say you feel awful, I wonder if you mean that you're feeling more sad in general, or if it's more a feeling of fear?"

"When you say awful, does that mean you're feeling upset with yourself or more upset with him... or is it something else?"

The idea, of course, is not to put words in people's mouths, but to work alongside them to *help them think and process their emotions*. Tact and care are essential.

Helping others identify their emotional triggers

What is an emotional trigger?

Though the word "trigger" has unfortunately become greatly overused in

recent years, it simply points to the human tendency to create associations between certain events, people, and feelings. When we make a connection between a random stimulus and the feeling we experienced the first time we encountered this stimulus, then it can act as a future trigger for us.

Remember in our example how the partner helpfully labelled your overwhelming emotion as "embarrassment"? This alone may be a powerful way to lower the emotional intensity and gain that all-important psychological distance. But, it could be taken further. *Why* did you react the way you did? People encounter customer service representatives on the phone all the time without ever feeling anything stronger than a slight annoyance. But you felt more. Why?

The answer may be that something triggered you. **The pre-existing associations in our own minds help us decide which situations count as threats.** Let's say you chat about it with your partner a little more (they're a very patient partner!) and through gentle questioning, they help you understand why you felt so especially riled up by this situation.

Let's say that because of your upbringing and your particular childhood experiences, you've come to feel especially sensitive to any situation where it looks like you're being judged for being overly emotional, inappropriate, or embarrassing to those around you. Let's say you had strict, formal parents who always quietly shamed any expression of exuberance. In your home, there were harsh penalties for raising your voice or expressing unhappiness. As an adult, you find any hint of this attitude very distressing.

Now, how can we ourselves become good at the kind of help this fictional partner was able to provide in this scenario?

Helping other people identify their own emotional triggers is a way to further help them emotionally regulate, gain awareness, and lower feelings of intensity and overwhelm. In the above example, realizing that you've been triggered instantly shifts the focus of the problem–it's not really the fault of the person on the phone at all. They're just doing their job, and it genuinely isn't personal. Knowing this, it's easier to process the anger, drop the bad feeling, and move on.

Helping someone else identify their own emotional triggers is really just helping them identify the real cause of the way they're feeling. A few things to note:

- This isn't always required of you, nor is it always appropriate. Though it's possible to

gently broach the "real cause" of someone else's emotion, helping others articulate triggers is usually best reserved for those we know well.
- We need to be fully aware of our own triggers and able to take ownership of them. Trying to talk about other people's triggers when we scarcely understand our own will likely result in confusion or hurtful misunderstandings.
- Finally, while it goes without saying, let's say it here: do not attempt to help someone identify their emotional triggers if that trigger is… you.

Very often, in conflicts and misunderstandings, people are unaware that they have been triggered and wrongly assume that the person or situation in front of them is to blame for their unpleasant feelings. This leads to attacks, judgment, or blame which only further escalates the problem. If the real source of the bad feeling can be identified, however, not only does this dampen hostile feelings, but it also gives people the opportunity to do something genuinely helpful to address the problem.

Being aware of emotional triggers can help you better understand someone, and it can also help you generate responses, suggestions, and interpretations that have a real chance of being insightful for them. Identifying triggers is innately validating because it paints a logical narrative: you behave like *this* because in the past, you behaved like *that*. There's a connection. It's understandable. It all *makes sense*. If nobody is really to "blame," then there is no further need to accuse or defend, right?

Psychoanalysis not required

A small warning here. You'll recall the importance of not placing our own interpretive filters over other peoples' lives, not making assumptions and judgments, and not putting words into their mouths. While it can be useful to help people identify their emotional triggers, our task is just that–to help *them* do it. Our own interpretations are not required.

Avoid the temptation to present other people with foregone conclusions about themselves, or to ask questions that are really just designed to funnel them along to a conclusion that you want them to reach. "Trigger talk" is everywhere these days, but the goal is not to go on the hunt for excuses or people to blame (for example, your mom's behavior twenty years ago is really the reason for your poor behavior today).

Rather, **identifying triggers is just a way to build more awareness of how our behavior**

patterns unfold over time. The more people understand about causes and effects in their automatic responses, the more they can consciously choose to step in and break that cycle. You don't need to become anyone's therapist; simply stay curious and keep asking questions.

Here are some non-judgmental ways to gently andcompassionately invite others to reflect on the triggers and causes of their own emotions:

Take note of strong reactions

Be alert for any reactions or emotional responses that seem disproportionate to the situation. Without judgment, notice any strong reactions that seem out of place, or sudden changes in behavior that don't seem connected to the present. Reactions that seem unusually strong can suggest that the person is not reacting to the situation at hand, but their own interpretation of that situation.

In a way that's appropriate, invite them to notice this, too, without making value judgments or assumptions about what it means.

"It seems like this thing in particular is really upsetting to you. Have you noticed that?"

"Your mood seems to have suddenly shifted... do you think so too?"

Work backwards

Become curious about what came directly before this exaggerated response. Triggers can be internal (thoughts, feelings, beliefs) or external (other people, places, words, activities, sensations, situations, even times of day). You could ask, "It seemed like you were OK a moment ago, and now you're not so OK. Have I got that right? I'm wondering what's happened between then and now."

Try to spot the trigger

It's not always obvious what the real trigger is–to anyone. But the act of deliberately looking at everything that came before will raise awareness, and insight will come with time. If you want this process to be validating for them, however, remember to be patient and use your questions and prompts to demonstrate your care, rather than prying into something they may not be ready to discuss.

Go gently and be tactful. If someone has come to you to vent, to get support, or to simply be reassured that they're not going crazy, then it may not be fitting to start prompting them to think of the "deeper causes" behind their reaction. They feel as they feel, and having you validate that can be enough. Likewise, be careful about suggesting that a reaction is "just" a trigger. If someone feels hurt, especially if they're upset at another person, jumping into psychological explanations can itself feel invalidating ("I don't want to talk about my childhood, I want to talk about what a jerk he is!").

Many people find that when it comes to unpacking triggers and making sense of more complex behavioral and emotional patterns, awareness comes slowly. You're not going to magically help someone solve all their problems in one conversation! But what you can do is listen closely, validate, and plant seeds of curiosity and acceptance that will blossom over time.

Using compliments

Throughout our book so far, we've just assumed there is obvious value in making someone feel accepted, recognized, acknowledged, and validated. But when you stop to think about it, what is the need we're actually meeting when we emotionally validate someone?

Deep down, **emotional validation is about confirming a human being's innate worth**. The whole reason it feels so good to be seen and heard is because this ultimately reaffirms our goodness and value as people.

If you've ever born witness to a nasty argument, then you'll know that sometimes, it's almost as though there are two conversations going on. There's the superficial, verbal one. This is where people are getting defensive, going on the attack, bluffing, explaining, boasting, obfuscating, blaming, and all the rest. This is the realm of conflict, and it's the realm where we *indirectly* attempt to meet our needs–and often fail.

But beneath this flows a second, invisible, more sincere "conversation." This is where our deep, real and unspoken energies, desires, and fears interact. This is the raw, emotional realm.

On the surface, it may look like Person A is nagging Person B about feeding the cat, to give a random example. But the second, hidden conversation would entail Person A begging, "Why does nobody listen to me? Am I not good enough or something?" and Person B responding continually, "I don't want to be responsible for making you happy! I'm scared of the size of your need!"

This may be an exaggeration–but only slightly! What if there was a way to directly address all of these needs, desires, and fears in the emotional realm? **What if there was a way to completely sidestep all people's defenses, walls and masks and speak directly to that**

part of them that simply wants to feel that they, as human beings, have innate worth? Well, it turns out there *is* a way to do this! This amazing technology is called a compliment.

In Solution-Focused Brief Therapy (SFBT), compliments in particular are a way to directly recognize and praise a person's strengths, achievements, and progress. Even beyond validating their emotions, we can validate them as people, and let them know that they are, in the broadest possible sense, good, valued, and appreciated for the unique contribution they bring to the world. In a way, this is the ultimate in "speaking the language of emotions" since we speak directly to people's inner being.

Compliments are about so much more than mere flattery or positive reinforcement (read: manipulation). A genuine, compassionate compliment is not about telling people that we specifically approve of them, but rather that they possess an absolute value that you are merely recognizing. A well-placed comment can be like gold dust. The good feelings it generates can lower people's defenses, dissolve tension, and strengthen connection faster than almost anything else.

However, there are a few things to keep in mind when using compliments for emotional validation:

Be genuine. Where possible, be spontaneous and don't fake it–a false compliment is worse than no compliment. Your recognition of them needs to be sincere.

Frame it as a question. One way to create the effect of a compliment without stirring any potential resistance is to frame it with curiosity. Ask, "Wow, how did you figure that out so fast?" Likewise, asking for someone's opinion, advice, or help on something that *they* (not you) consider themselves skilled at will really make them feel special.

Prompt them to self-compliment. You can invite other people to notice something they're doing that's worth praise and recognition. "What did you bring to the table that made the project such a success?"

Less is more. A single sincere compliment is more than enough. Don't lay it on too thick or you risk arousing suspicion!

Compliment on the right things. It's usually a good idea to praise people for their hard work and effort, for their endurance, patience, and other virtues, and specifically for the things you know that they value (even if you don't personally value those things). Avoid complimenting them on things they have no control over, or things you can't be sure they consider significant. Especially avoid compliments that could be interpreted as introducing pressure, expectations, or assumptions. (For example, "You'll make an amazing wife one day!")

Sincerity is sometimes enough. Finally, don't feel you need to be especially clever in your compliment. Sometimes, simplicity and sincerity count the most. A five-year-old tells his mother, "I'm so glad you exist." It's the best compliment she's ever received in her life.

Summary

- It's common to disregard our own feelings and the feelings of others, but becoming emotionally literate means learning to switch gears and pay more attention to the world of emotion.
- An important skill is emotional acknowledgement, which means noticing someone's emotional state and expressing it verbally. Recognizing and acknowledging emotions in this way can be profoundly validating.
- Emotional acknowledgement and labeling benefits everyone; even incorrectly

labelling an emotion is better than ignoring it completely.
- What matters is effort, care, and the intention to connect, but there is also value in putting precise words to emotions. Affect labeling helps people emotionally regulate, cope, and better understand themselves. We can help others find psychological distance and more self-awareness, but we ourselves need to be aware and emotionally literate. If you can name it, you can tame it!
- Triggers are pre-existing associations in our minds that help us interpret events in the present, causing emotions. Thoughtful questions can help people reflect on the deeper causes and origins of their emotions and behaviors. Without psychoanalyzing, try to build awareness of how behavior patterns unfold over time, and where they come from.
- Finally, use appropriate, meaningful compliments to praise people and remind them of their innate worth–it's the direct road to validation.

Chapter 3: Become a Master of Empathetic Listening

Imagine that in front of you right now is an old friend who is talking at length about a troubling situation they're going through. As they talk, it's a mix of them recounting events, retelling their reactions, making conjectures about what it all means, and asking rhetorical questions–plus the occasional emotional outburst.

As you listen, you become aware of the fact that they've been talking for a while, and clearly need to "vent." Then your thoughts start to wander. "Ah ha! This is one of *those* situations. Here's my chance to practice this whole active listening thing. What should I do to show them I'm listening and that their emotions are valid…?"

Soon feeling very conscious of your own virtue and mindfulness, you give a few thoughtful nods and "uh-huh" sounds, adopt a concerned expression, and even say "wow, that sounds hard." now and then.

You think to yourself, "Damn, I'm good at this. I'm being *so* empathetic right now. I bet they feel really seen and heard. This stuff's a breeze!" Then you start mentally formulating the extremely intelligent and wise response you'll be kind enough to offer them just as soon as they stop talking ... Then they too will see just how incredibly insightful and helpful you are...

"Are you even listening to me?" your friend says, interrupting your reverie.

Well, where you?

When we listen, we validate

Much of the guidance out there on how to be better listener makes the same fatal error: it confuses *listening* with the *appearance of listening*. The advice is usually sound – we are told to make eye contact, to not interrupt, to nod and mirror our facial expressions and body language, to ask questions, and so on.

Those are all good things, aren't they? Yes, but the reality is that these things are the *result of* active and empathetic listening. They are not the same thing as listening, and they certainly do not *cause* it, as our example at the opening of this chapter shows. If you've ever been stuck in conversation with someone who clearly thought they were doing a good job listening, but weren't, then you'll know exactly how important it is to make the distinction!

Throughout this chapter we will consider various theories, models, and concepts to help us finetune our own listening skills. However, it's worth remembering that all of these **techniques and methods mean little if they don't stem from an attitude of genuine receptivity and interest in other people**. This mindset is the root of authentic listening skills.

So, what exactly is this mindset? The core of it is validation, namely our ability and readiness to see that other people, and the things they have to say, matter.

It's a mindset that does not see the act of listening as a generous favor we offer to other people, out of our own goodness and superiority. It does not view listening as difficult or a sacrifice. Rather, our ability to fully pay attention to, accept, and validate other people's emotions is something we are sincerely interested in–even to the point of considering it a privilege!

If you consistently held this attitude, then all the recommended behaviors will naturally follow. Without this attitude, all the right behaviors will come across as false. This is why we'll begin our chapter with the biggest and most important skill to cultivate: a real interest in other people. If ever you find yourself feeling bored, frustrated or confused by other people, remind yourself that everyone you meet has something fascinating and genuinely valuable to teach you.

Active listening versus empathetic listening

Not unlike Marsha Linehan's levels of validation, there are different levels of listening. These levels range from not listening at all, to very superficial listening, to passive listening, all the way to deeper forms of active and empathetic listening–the forms we're most interested in. Both active listening and empathetic listening are useful communication skills to learn, but they serve quite distinct purposes. How are they different, and how do we use each in different contexts?

Active listening is where we purposefully concentrate our attention on what someone is saying, engage with the content

of their words, and demonstrate this engagement through our own verbal and nonverbal responses. We do all the right things–like asking questions and paraphrasing what we've heard–because our empathy tells us that these things will make the other person feel acknowledged and validated (Hybels & Weaver, 2015).

Taking things further, however, is the use of **empathetic listening** which, as you can guess, **entails engaging more deeply with the emotional content of what's being shared.** This is where emotional validation comes into play. We are not just hearing the facts, words, and *informational content* of a message, but recognizing, validating, and responding to the *emotional content* of that message, too.

Going through the motions and giving the appearance of being a good listener may be sufficient if we stay on the more superficial listening levels. But if we wish to go any deeper, and to engage in real empathetic listening, then we need to adopt a genuine mindset shift in how we view other people.

Prominent humanistic psychologist Carl Rogers believed that empathetic listening is a way of really connecting to someone's humanity, entering fully into their world, and encountering them without judgment. He felt that listening of this type can only be done emotionally and, importantly, it can't be faked. The all-important connection needs to be based on "unconditional positive regard" and respect for the other person.

Thinking honestly about your own life, when was the last time you practiced this kind of deep listening?

While active listening entails a few useful "tips and tricks", empathetic listening stems from a more all-encompassing mindset, and a collection of beliefs, namely:

- People are important and deserving of respect, care, and understanding.
- People are interesting and we can learn from them.
- People are valid.
- People can be different from us–and that's not only OK, but welcome.

Such a mindset also sees communication and relationships in a particular way:

- A conversation is a joint creation.
- The most important thing is connection, not content.
- Speaking is not necessarily more desirable than listening.
- A conversation is not a battleground, a stage, a court of law, a pulpit, or a

lecture hall–it's a place where we connect to one another.

Covey's 4 stages of empathetic listening

According to Steve Covey, author of popular self-help book *The 7 Habits of Highly Effective People*, there are four stages of empathetic listening. See if you can identify the areas of overlap with other models covered so far.

Stage 1: Repeating or mimicking content

This is the most superficial kind of listening, and least likely to spur real connection. To show we are listening, we literally repeat the facts of what we've heard. (Note, this is not the same as affective labeling, which is focused on emotions.)

Stage 2: Paraphrasing

Here we show that we have heard the message, but also that we have actually understood it, and we confirm that what we've received is factually accurate.

Stage 3: Reflecting

This is going a step further and observing and acknowledging how the speaker themselves feels about the facts of the situation. Here, emotion begins to enter the picture; responding to the emotional content of the message means we can "say the unspoken part out loud."

Stage 4: Rephrasing and reflecting feelings

This stage is a mix of the second and third stages: we rephrase and reflect, especially the emotional content. Covey explains this as giving someone "psychological air," or a space to explore and unfold their experience. The result is improved trust, understanding, intimacy, and connection.

Whether Covey's theory resonates with you or not, you can probably see that it too traces a progression towards deeper sincerity and understanding, rather than just the rote, outward manifestations of understanding.

Now, this isn't to say that the "best" form of listening is always the deepest and fullest, or that you are required to offer every person your fullest possible engagement. Recall that listening and entering into someone's world incurs its own psychological cost, and we would deplete ourselves quickly if we used deep listening in every circumstance. In fact, later in our book we'll explore some situations where empathetic listening and validation are definitely not recommended-but more on that later.

The knowledge underlying these various theories and models is the recognition that **not all listening is equal**. We need to know *how* and *when* to apply different forms.

In casual and superficial situations, less intense mimicry and reflection are perfectly appropriate. More serious situations will demand all the empathetic listening you can muster–and usually more!

No matter how you listen, however, every social interaction is an opportunity to demonstrate emotional validation, respect, concern, and acknowledgement. With a complete stranger, this may take the form of low-key warmth, politeness, and tact. With a work colleague it may look like more structured and deliberate dialogue; and with a loved one or dear friend it may look like a very raw and vulnerable conversation lasting many hours. Even passive listening or the mere illusion of listening can be appropriate, if it's the kindest option given the circumstances.

All of these expressions of respect for the speaker's humanity and worth are valid, but they necessarily vary in their intensity. Our challenge is to understand the many different ways we can manifest a truly compassionate attitude, so that we can choose the correct one for each unique situation.

The art of holding space

As we saw in our opening example, it is seldom enough to merely give the appearance of listening. If we are just sitting quietly, not really listening and merely waiting for our "turn" to speak, then we have failed to connect on any level, and are merely engaging in a kind of conversational tug of war.

The empathetic listener is one who understands, on a deep level, that conversation is a vehicle meant to truly meet and encounter other human beings. It is not an opportunity to merely meet their own needs. The purpose of conversation is not to argue your point, impress others, convince them, lecture them, or extract feelings of validation from them.

"Holding space" is a common therapy term that simply points to the creation of a platform that **centers the speaker**. When we hold space for someone, we are deliberately making it possible for them to share and express themselves. In this space, they are validated without judgment and without someone else trying to commandeer the conversation to their own ends.

The term was first popularized in a viral 2015 blog post by writer Heather Plett, where she described the power of "being willing to walk alongside another person in whatever journey they're on, without judging them, making them feel inadequate, trying to fix them, or trying to impact the outcome." You can read more in Plett's book, *The Art of Holding Space: A practice of love, liberation, and leadership* (2020, Page Two Books).

We can now recognize that all this is none other than the skill we've been exploring all along–the ability to enter someone's world and validate what we find there, without foisting our own assumptions, judgments, and interpretations onto it. Holding space, then, is creating an environment in which the other person can shine. That means that *we* need to get out of the way!

The "space" we're talking about is a psychological one, but it's also a literal, physical space. That's because it's not possible to have a proper conversation with anyone if the surrounding environment is uncomfortable or full of distractions. It may seem strange to say, but one of the most crucial listening skills you can develop is simply knowing *when* and *where* to hold a conversation in the first place.

Here are a few things to be mindful of.

How to create a space conducive to listening

- **Remove distractions.** Obvious distractions include TVs, phones, and other screens, as well as annoying sounds, noises, and interruptions. Think about any mental and emotional distractions, too, such as unfinished tasks or deadlines that may be "hanging over" a conversation. Also consider the presence of other people, and try to ensure complete privacy. Not everyone will find the same things distracting, of course. For some, talking while walking is fine and even makes opening up easier. For others, having to navigate a path adds more tension and distraction.
- **Remove obstacles to vulnerability**. Judgment is the biggest obstacle and prevents people from sharing honestly. Our own views, biases, opinions, and assumptions can get in the way long before they can be classified as judgments! Temporarily set aside your own reactions and feelings on the topic at hand, so that you can more clearly see theirs. The other person needs to feel that they can speak freely, without someone else making it all about them.
- **Remove excess noise.** Silence is a powerful tool when it comes to listening,

and not just for obvious reasons. We'll discuss how to use silence in the next section.

- **Remove uncertainty.** Pick a time and day to talk so you can get mentally prepared. Choose a location that works, and have clear expectations about how much time is available.
- **Remove the need to respond, to fix things, or to repress.** It can be difficult to talk to someone when we can sense they might shy away from difficult topics or be unwilling to face certain emotions. Everyone has limits, of course, but we need to be aware of how our own avoidance around certain topics can be felt to be invalidating. Try not to hijack people's space–even if you're trying to skip ahead to a helpful solution!
- **Remove risk.** Or, we should say, *reduce* risk. Too many people are afraid of sharing what they really feel because deep down, they predict that they will be punished somehow for doing so, or that their disclosure will indirectly cost them something. Good listeners will not make people regret opening up, they will not consider them indebted, nor will they use their vulnerability against them.

What's the opposite of holding space? That would be something like *hogging* space–and it's way more common than we'd like to admit! This behavior can creep in quickly, and includes:

- Jumping in to share an anecdote or story that relates to what you've heard... except it's about you.
- Repeatedly offering advice, solutions, or general "explanations" that center you and your opinion as the main frame of reference.
- Allowing your own emotions, responses, and opinions to dominate.
- Acting disinterested or disengaged until the speaker just runs out of steam from lack of reaction.
- Finally–the most obvious one–interrupting.

One way to think of it is to simply become aware of where attention is currently falling. **If we're trying to listen empathetically to someone, then the attention should be on them.** Any attempt on our behalf to snatch back that attention and place it on ourselves is likely to break the space and change the conversational dynamic. We need to center them, not ourselves.

When you can't (or don't want to) hold space

At this point you may be wondering, "Wow, this sounds so boring–they get to be the center of attention, and I just sit on the sidelines the whole time? What's in it for me?"

If you find yourself thinking this, it's a good sign that you're still inside the mindset that sees conversational attention as a limited resource over which people should compete. From this perspective, listening is an innately inferior position to "getting" to speak. But what's so bad about centering others, at the end of the day? Do we really lose anything by setting our own perspectives aside? After all, we can also pick it right back up again when we're done!

Of course, this is a guide about how to become a better listener, so that's the skill we're focusing on. You don't need to become a doormat, a lay therapist or everyone's eternal sounding board. At the root of an unwillingness to hold space for people can be the very real fear that extending this kindness and attention to others means it will be taken advantage of. People will just talk and talk and talk and we'll regret being so accommodating, right?

My suggestion would be to challenge this prediction and try it out for yourself. You may discover that the opposite is true–that it's only when people feel fully seen and heard that they are emotionally capable of relaxing and "sharing the limelight." Truly listen to someone, and you may see just how ready they are to do the same for you. Get caught in a conversational tug of war, though, and you may find that no matter how much you speak, the other person doesn't *want* to hear you, and why should they? You didn't listen to them.

That said, there are of course situations where offering space and attention are simply not appropriate or possible. Likewise, if you're feeling unwell, distracted, or emotionally unable, there's absolutely nothing wrong with making it clear that you can't engage with people in that way. My hope is that, if it's *you* that needs to share, you will seek out someone who is able to hold space for you.

Holding space for people, validating them, recognizing their stories, and practicing that powerful, unconditional regard is a wonderful thing to do for others, but you don't *have to* do it in order to be a good person or show that you care. If somebody's needs outstrip your ability to support and bear witness, it's OK to help by referring them to properly trained mental health professionals.

The power of silence

One of the most impactful things you can do in any conversation is say nothing.

By creating *aural space*, you communicate so much:

- "I'm not interested in jumping in with my own contribution."
- "I want to hear what you say, and I welcome it."
- "I want to give you space to reflect, process, and pause."
- "I respect that you may need time to say what you want to say."
- "This is not about me and my opinions."
- "I'm not in any rush, and I don't have any agenda."
- "I want you to direct the pace of this conversation."
- "I'm paying very close attention to everything you're saying."
- "I'm also willing to just *be here* with you, without having to talk."

If we remember that paying someone attention is intrinsically validating, then we can see that giving them this full attention, without doing anything to fill that space, extends that validation even further.

In therapy, psychologists and counsellors can make skillful use of silence as a rhetorical tool, and use it to invite and encourage deeper engagement and exploration of feelings. **The irony is that too much talk and chatter can sometimes make it *harder* for people to say what they mean**. Without the opportunity to regularly pause and absorb what is being said, it can a little like blasting along at full speed, never quite taking in what has transpired. We may even do this to ourselves, when we fill our own heads with self-talk instead of staying present with how we actually feel in the moment!

If silence is so wonderful, why don't more of us make use of it?

There can be many reasons. We may have been socialized to think of silence as awkward or even a sign that something is wrong and that the conversation is failing. We may hold unconscious beliefs that it's our job to always say something useful, to entertain people, to justify ourselves or to always be moving things along somehow. In many ways, too much talk can be an insidious coping mechanism that helps us avoid facing strong emotions head on.

But it's also true that, as a rule, people tend to seriously dislike silence. A recent study found that the unspoken rules around silences in conversations are fairly universal (Stiver at. Al., 2019). The researchers considered cultures from five different continents and ten different languages, and found that the gap between one person speaking and another speaking is just *200 milliseconds*!

This tells us that when most people talk, there is close to zero silence in the conversation. It also tells us that each speaker must be planning what to say before the other has finished speaking, or else be blurting out their contributions without thinking. Could *you* think up a carefully considered response in just 200 milliseconds?

Stiver and her team settled on what they considered to be two universal rules in conversation, namely that people tend not to talk at the same time, and people also tend not to leave big empty spaces between "turns." Big gaps, they claim, may signal disagreement or disengagement. All this is to say that most of us have a strong tendency to want to avoid silences at all costs.

However, even though it may feel a tiny bit awkward at first, if you can resist the urge to fill up that space, you may discover that just 10 or 15 seconds can immediately deepen a conversation and create more trust and intimacy. In fact, being willing to break this conversational convention can itself be a signal: "We are no longer in the realm of chit-chat and small talk. We are now having a more authentic engagement."

In the therapy room, the anxiety triggered by silence becomes an interesting provocation that the therapist can use to build awareness. But in our everyday lives, as people who merely want to be better listeners, our willingness to be silent can signal the willingness to shift the conversation towards more authenticity–and that shift alone can be validating.

Silence is not "empty" space–there's a lot going on when people are silent! (Knol et. al., 2020). Silence lets conversations breathe and take the shape they need to. It acts like punctuation, encouraging us to slow down, and be more present with what is actually happening. Silence can be sympathetic, attentive, and highly dynamic. Bear in mind also that we can keep verbally quiet while still sharing a rich *nonverbal* message–for example through our facial expressions, eye contact, body language etc.

In our quest to learn to better emotionally validate others, there are a few ways to use silence during conversations.

Notice meaningful pauses

During the flow of conversation, pay attention to abrupt shifts in energy. Is there a sudden change in tempo, in the volume or pitch of the voice, in the content? More importantly, can you observe a change in the emotion being expressed?

As we've seen before, strong emotional reactions can signal the work of a trigger, but a more subtle indication that something is going on is when the person pauses. A gap in speech may suggest that they're processing, thinking, or even wrestling internally. When they stop speaking externally, it may reveal that they've started to speak to themselves *internally*!

Not every pause is deep and meaningful, but notice if people suddenly drop their gaze downwards, or appear to be biting their tongue. The pause itself is significant, but the meaning may be revealed upon considering *where* that pause falls:

"Are you happy in your job?"

"I'm... I'm not unhappy."

What happened during that long pause? What decisions, appraisals, and considerations were being made? What did the person consciously choose *not* to say?

Paying attention to pauses is one way of reading between the lines. Simply notice what these pauses might mean given the context. In terms of validation, recognize these pauses and respect them. If you mirror their pause or silence, you allow them the time and space to process.

Notice inarticulation

Have you ever noticed how, when you're feeling emotionally overwhelmed, it can be difficult to put things into words? Notice when this happens with other people. Pauses are silences, but we can also consider hesitation, stumbling over words, and general inarticulation as a kind of silence.

A person fumbling and second-guessing out loud ("It's a frustrating job... well I'm not frustrated, maybe I'm just a little bored? Or tired? I don't know...") may be wrestling with strong emotions. Depending on the context, they may also be revealing strong secondary emotions, for example guilt for feeling angry, confusion about feeling bored, or anger about feeling sad.

If you notice someone fumbling this way, it can be tempting to jump in and offer an emotion label–but try to hold off for as long as you can! Don't rush them or put words in their mouths. Your silence is what will allow them to gather their thoughts and find their own clarity.

Listen to body language, too

Sometimes a pause is just a pause, and a silence means nothing. But if it's paired with anxious or uncomfortable body language, it probably reveals some unspoken emotion. Often, people who are experiencing strong emotions that they don't want to experience will show nonverbal signs of "holding back" or "holding on"–they will tightly clench their fists, set their jaws, or lock their bodies into rigid positions. Silence can be a big part of this response, potentially revealing an unwillingness or inability to acknowledge or endure an emotion.

If you notice someone clamming up this way, validate what they're feeling by not adding any more tension. Respect the silence and let them be the first ones to break it. Later, if it feels appropriate, you might make an observation like, "I noticed back there that you seemed a bit tense. What's on your mind?"

Silences can be understood as a kind of behavior, and as an empathetic listener, you can learn to observe this behavior and commit to acknowledging and respecting it when you see it. Most people have been socialized to spot silences and quickly rush to fill them. But when a person pauses, they are signaling that they are dealing with an emotion–even if it's just a small one. **When we respect and mirror that silence, we are showing that we respect and validate the emotion behind it.**

Listening for emotional metaphors

Imagine you're speaking again to the same friend who is having problems in their job. They say, "I can't find the word for things. I don't know how I feel. I'm being pulled in two directions, and I'm so torn. On the one hand, I know the promotion is a real achievement, but on the other... I don't know. I thought I really wanted the new role, but instead everything seems like it's unraveling...!"

Now, nowhere in this description has your friend said a single emotion word. Yet, you probably know exactly what they're talking about, right?

Despite claiming not to be able to find the words for things, your friend has offered some deeply descriptive metaphors to explain their situation: they're being pulled apart, almost literally, by two opposing feelings. This is a real tug-of-war metaphor, and the mention of hands further emphasizes the tension of being caught in the middle–your friend is possibly the metaphorical rope between these two opposing forces. And that rope is unraveling!

Emotional metaphors are extremely powerful, and most of us are so familiar with using them that we're not even always aware they're there.

"She was really cold to me."

"I'm bursting with new ideas!"

"There's just a shadow over everything now…"

"Am I'm just a slave to this thing?"

"The situation has really shaken me to my core."

"I'm lost."

"I've gotten really tangled up."

"I feel like I've been sleepwalking through this whole relationship."

"Something in me died that day."

"I feel they've set traps for me at every corner."

The emotional symbols found in these metaphors help bring structure to shapeless internal sensations, and allow us to communicate them in ways that others can intuitively understand. A good metaphor can even induce the same feeling in the listener, and directly provoke the listener's sympathy. Emotional metaphors that reference the body, for example, point to things we can all relate to. It's as though, when someone says, "It was a punch to the gut." or "My knees went weak," we know exactly what they mean because we can guess how that would feel in our own bodies. Such metaphors create a kind of "embodied empathy."

How can we use metaphors to better validate someone's emotional experience? That's simple: listen closely for, and reflect, their metaphorical language.

For example, if someone has expressed their mood in terms of *shadows*, you may acknowledge and validate this metaphor by asking a little more about the "light" in their life that is being dimmed, or about dark places. You might choose to frame solutions in terms of sunniness and brightness. Done well, adopting someone's symbolic language in this way will make the interaction feel natural and comfortable.

The reverse is also true: if we subtly ignore or even contradict someone's emotional metaphor, we may be perceived to be invalidating the emotion that inspired it. To return to the first example, your friend is talking about being torn between two feelings, but if you jump in and introduce an unrelated metaphor ("It's always darkest before the dawn.") they will rightly feel that you haven't understood them.

Listening for emotional content

There exists an emotional dimension rich in significance and meaning. The information in this dimension is always available to whomever is willing to pay attention to it. Noticing symbolic and metaphorical language is an easy way to gain access to this dimension, and can help the skilled listener detect patterns and hidden connections that might not otherwise be apparent.

In fact, the use of metaphoric language may actually increase when people are experiencing strong emotions, so the simple presence of such metaphors alone is a big clue. Lakoff and Johnson (1980) theorize that this happens precisely because metaphors express and organize our thinking so well. Metaphors are culturally recognized cognitive tools that quickly and concisely convey our emotional experiences to others.

It stands to reason that if someone is experiencing a strong emotion, and they resort to using metaphorical language, they are doing so in an attempt to clearly express themselves and communicate that emotion. Why? The point of a metaphor is to inspire understanding. It's not a leap to say that metaphorical language, then, is actually *a bid for emotional validation.*

This is why **it can be so powerful to hear, validate, and reflect the metaphors people use.** In doing so, we send the deep message: "I've heard you. Your language makes sense. I know the emotions you're talking about. I get it. I get *you*."

Unfortunately, many people have been led to believe that metaphorical language is somehow not as valuable as factual, objective language. Because it is imprecise, we may feel that we need to go in and clarify, and if the feeling is coded in metaphor, we may assume it's our job to translate it into more acceptable language.

The power of a metaphor is indeed paradoxical. How can we better understand a thing by describing all the things it factually isn't? However, the emotional realm does work this way, and this form of expression has its own legitimacy.

Metaphors point to deeper truths in the human heart, even if they do so indirectly. This is why it would be a mistake to ignore or even correct metaphorical language. Instead, the most validating response is to stay within the metaphor (Villatte et. al., 2014, *The Big book of*

ACT Metaphors: The Complete Guide to ACT Metaphors and Experiential Exercises).

Here are two practical ways to do just that:

Notice the metaphor, and acknowledge it through mirroring and reflection

Pay close attention to symbolic language (you'll be surprised at how much of it there is!) and show your acknowledgement by reflecting it back to the speaker. The easiest way to do this is to continue to use the same imagery, words, and descriptors.

They may say, "I have the weight of the world on my shoulders!" and you could reflect that emotion by saying, "Wow, that's heavy. What a burden that must be."

Stay inside the metaphor

By continuing to talk within that symbolic framework, you are helping people to think through and process their emotions. Asking open-ended questions can encourage further exploration of the feelings that inspired the metaphor. If it seems appropriate, you can take things a step further and begin to explore alternative perspectives and ideas, all within the same metaphorical universe. Take a look at the following responses to some of our earlier examples:

"I'm torn. I'm being pulled in two different directions."

Response: "Who do you think is doing the pulling?"

"I'm carrying the weight of the world on my shoulders!"

Response: "Do you ever wonder what it would be like to put that burden down for a moment?"

"I feel like I've been sleepwalking through this whole relationship."

Response: "What would it take to wake up?"

"I feel like they've set traps for me at every corner."

Response: "That sounds really nerve wracking. I mean, what happens if you get caught in a trap?"

According to therapist Alwin Wagener, **metaphors are "linked to how individuals process information and emotions"** (*Metaphor in Professional Counseling*, 2017). If we can understand how people are processing their own experience, how they're thinking, and what meaning they're making of the world, then we give ourselves a precious glimpse into their very being. What's more, we can reflect these insights back to them as they open up and share how they feel, hopefully triggering greater self-awareness in them.

Once you start paying attention to metaphorical language, it's a little like discovering a secret language that's been there all along. Learn to decipher these messages, and every social interaction comes alive in a special way.

Active constructive responding

When we are aware of the emotional content in the messages people are communicating, then we empower ourselves to respond to that information and validate it. If we respond merely to the verbal content, we may miss out on an opportunity for genuine connection and understanding. Bearing in mind that most of us express emotions because we crave recognition of those feelings, ignoring this need in others can lead to feelings of rupture and disconnection. We are listening… but we're not really *listening*.

Here's an example to show just how that rupture and disconnect can creep in when we don't listen to the whole message. Imagine that one day you suddenly find $100 just lying on the floor. Later that day you tell a friend about your good luck, smiling and laughing and wondering out loud what you'll spend it on. Your friend doesn't smile back at you. In fact, they just say, "Oh. You've got to feel sorry for the poor person who lost it, but... good for you, I guess."

There's no doubt that this response is invalidating, but why? The answer is that your friend has not validated your emotions–happiness and excitement. In fact, they've barely even acknowledged them, and the response feels almost like an attack. This is a destructive response, and you can see why. Your unspoken emotional message was "I'm excited!" and their unspoken emotional response was "You shouldn't be." The relationship may feel like it takes a knock.

Psychologist Shelly Gable first introduced the concept of Active Constructive Responding, or ACR. This is a method of engaging with the emotional content of the messages people share with us, and it's ultimately all about validation. Gable explains how **responses can be either active or passive, and they can be either constructive (builds the connection up) or destructive (damages the connection).**

This yields four broad possibilities, as follows:

Passive constructive – validating, but low energy and low effort. May entail a response that is dampened, delayed, subdued, or insufficient.

All your dreams have come true? "Oh, that's nice."

You've had the worst day of your entire life? "Huh. Poor thing. Sounds tough."

Passive destructive –invalidating as well as low energy and low effort. Could entail an attempt to pull attention away from the speaker, avoid the topic or conversation, engage in passive aggression, ignore the speaker, or change the topic.

You share an awkward and difficult piece of news, and they say, "Cool. What's for dinner?"

You announce your long-awaited engagement. They say, "Oh. I've been married almost ten years."

Active destructive – more effortful and deliberate; a response that intentionally demeans, undermines, dismisses, or invalidates the unspoken emotion.

In response to your genuine fear and terror, they laugh and say, "Ha! Are you seriously this much of a wuss? Don't be ridiculous, it'll be fine!"

Responding to your happy news, they scoff and frown: "You've won the lottery? Oh my god, you'd better watch out. Money only causes trouble. But then you've always been materialistic…"

Active constructive – the most validating and connection-affirming response, where the listener matches the emotional energy that they perceive (good or bad) and reflect its intensity.

If you're scared, or unhappy, or have a bad day, they respond with eye contact, concern, interest, and a willingness to reflect your emotion: "Oh man, this all sounds so overwhelming. You must be finding it so difficult, I'm sorry. Want to talk?"

If you're happy or excited, they reflect this, too: "Hooray! Fantastic news! I'm so pleased for you. Tell me more, I want to hear all about it…"

As you can see, we are not classifying responses as "negative" or "positive," but rather we are characterizing them on whether they validate, recognize, and support the expressed emotion… or not. This is an important distinction to make, because sometimes we think we're being supportive when we respond to someone's unhappiness or discomfort with forceful positivity.

Responding *actively* means we are alert, engaged, and willing to expend energy and emotional resources on the connection.

Responding *constructively* means we respond in a way that respects and upholds the other person's message, protects our shared relationship, and validates and mirrors their underlying emotion. **When listeners can respond to speakers actively and constructively, it makes both parties feel better, and it supports and strengthens their bond** (Lambert et al., 2013).

It's not just about negative emotions

Conventional psychology has tended to focus on the best way to respond to people who are sharing negative emotions. Gable and her fellow researchers, however, have learned that how we respond to positive emotions matters, too.

Perhaps you know of someone who is an amazingly supportive friend, but nevertheless seems a little cool or aloof when you're *not* having an emotional crisis. For many complex reasons, it may feel easier for us and less threatening to support and validate people when they're feeling low than when they're really happy. However, the way we respond to people when they're feeling good reveals far more about us and the nature of our relationship with them.

Active constructive responses to positive emotion can create a kind of upward spiral of good feelings and positivity. By acknowledging the best in people (rather than merely supporting them at their worst) we are practicing an underrated version of validation. **Emotional validation should not be reserved for negative emotions only, it should include all emotions.**

Here are some additional ways to start cultivating more active and constructive responses:

Be honest about your response style

Overall, how do you tend to respond to positive emotions in others? What about negative ones? Think about the last time you responded to someone's news and ask how passive/active you were, and whether your response built up your connection, or damaged it. The more aware you are of your own patterns and tendencies, the more you'll be able to consider healthier alternatives.

Try to match and reflect emotion

Sharing an emotion with someone who doesn't reflect it back to us can be as disconcerting as looking into a mirror and seeing a face you don't recognize. You don't have to literally feel the same as they do, but visibly mirroring their emotion back to them is a basic form of empathy and validation. Is their tone of voice high pitched? Raise yours a little, too. Are they slouched and not saying much? Adopt a similar posture and match their quietness.

Be genuinely happy for others

It may not be flattering to admit, but sometimes the happiness of other people can feel like a threat. We may not even realize our own tendency to quietly undermine them, to dampen their spirits, or to quickly jump in with a "realistic" interpretation that knocks the wind out of their sails. This is subtle but toxic behavior that will erode trust and closeness over time.

When a friend is unhappy, we may not feel bad ourselves, but we can respect and acknowledge that it's how they feel. The same is true for positive emotions. *We* may not be feeling totally happy in that moment, but that doesn't mean that their happiness isn't valid.

Be curious and engaged

Passive constructive responses can arguably be the worst because they're *almost* right – but they nevertheless leave people feeling unimportant, unheard, or unloved. Make an effort to do more than just acknowledge someone's emotion. Instead of being passive, be curious. Ask meaningful follow-up questions, show an interest, and do what you can to engage further.

Summary

- When trying to be more empathetic listeners, we need to remember that *listening* is not the same as the *appearance of listening*. Supportive verbal and nonverbal responses are great, but techniques mean little if they don't stem from an attitude of genuine receptivity and interest in other people.
- Active listening is concentrating our attention on the content of people's words, whereas empathetic listening is engaging more deeply with the emotional content of the message. We need to see people as inherently valuable, and our connection with them as a cherished means of connection.
- Not all listening is equal; we need to match the intensity of our listening and validation to the circumstances.
- Conversation is a vehicle to connect with others, not merely meet our own needs. Holding literal and psychological space means creating opportunities to center the speaker. Try to remove distractions, obstacles to vulnerability, judgment, and noise, and instead create safety and trust.

It's also OK to not hold space for others if we feel unable.
- One of the most impactful things you can do in any conversation is say nothing. Silence is not "empty" space. Respect and reflect people's silences to give them time to process.
- Listen closely for emotional metaphors and use the same language to signal understanding and validation.
- Finally, practice active constructive responding to match the emotional content of people's messages. Seek to build up the connection and validate the emotion behind all emotions people share with you.

Chapter 4: What Not to Do

We've spent the last few chapters exploring in some detail what validation is, and how to bring it into our connections with others. But it's also worth seeing things from the other side, too–i.e. exploring all the things that validation *is not.*

Offering genuine validation is not always easy, obvious, or automatic. Most of the time, if/when we invalidate someone, it's not because we're bad people or we don't really care about them. Rather, it's simply because we're distracted or accidentally invalidating them because we want to help.

In this chapter we're looking at exactly what constitutes an invalidating response (and it's not always what you think!) as well as considering the trap of toxic positivity. We'll look at the best kind of advice to give (hint:

usually the best advice is no advice) as well as the art of revealing a little of yourself as others share themselves with you.

<u>Emotionally invalidating responses</u>

Recall the purpose of validation: it's to communicate to other people that their feelings are reasonable and make sense, that we recognize and accept them as legitimate.

To invert this, then, **invalidation is sending the message that people's feelings are unreasonable and don't make sense, and that we don't recognize them as legitimate.**

That definition probably sounds quite harsh, but in real life, invalidating statements may slip out of our mouths really easily, without us necessarily thinking we're being mean at all:

Dismissing, minimizing:

- "Well, it could be much worse"
- "Don't worry about it"
- "Well, what can you do? That's life"
- "You think *that's* bad?"

Judging the emotion:

- "You're overreacting / taking this too seriously / blowing this out of proportion"
- "Just calm down / relax"

- "You're being difficult / ridiculous / unfair / weird"
- "You're too sensitive"

Forcing interpretations:

- "These things happen for a reason"
- "Suffering is just an illusion"
- "Try to see the good in the experience"
- "Your problem is your lack of self-esteem"
- "Time to find your anger!"

Blaming:

- "But you could have avoided this"
- "You always get yourself in these messes"
- "Why do you do this to yourself?"

Centering yourself, giving advice:

- "You should just try yoga"
- "You have got to get a divorce"
- "I wouldn't have done that"
- "I don't see the problem, personally"

Undermining their reason and judgment:

- "I'm sure you've just misunderstood"
- "It's not *really* that bad"
- "Are you sure you're not imagining things?"
- "There are two sides to every story."

Have you ever uttered any of the above? Chances are, you weren't really intending to be invalidating; you were probably just engaging in the knee-jerk reaction most of us have now and then to people who express negative emotion. We may be extremely kind and compassionate people, but there is just something about the appearance of strong or unpleasant emotions that invites a little pushback–especially if those emotions catch us by surprise or hit a little close to home.

These examples may seem obvious, and of course they are, given without context. **In real life, invalidation is often far more subtle** and can be particularly damaging because people *feel* invalidated... but they don't know why, or where that feeling is coming from. The person doing the invalidation may be just as unaware of what's happened.

To illustrate this point, take a look at this exchange between a father and his 8-year-old daughter.

"Dad, the other girls at school keep saying I'm ugly."

"What?! Oh honey, that's ridiculous. You're not ugly. You're beautiful."

"No I'm not. I'm ugly."

"No. You. Are. Not. I *never* want to hear you say that again, OK? You're beautiful, do you understand?"

Now, does this father care deeply about his daughter and want to do everything he can to help her? Of course. Is he sincere? Absolutely. Is he emotionally invalidating? Sadly, yes.

Our most invalidating responses can sometimes come from a good place. We see something in others that we don't like and are uncomfortable with (in this case, the heartbreaking idea that an 8-year-old thinks she's ugly) and we allow our own emotional reactions to take over.

However, in this father's attempt to help, he has actually doubled his daughter's misery. Now, she feels bad because she has been insulted by the other children, but she *also* feels bad because she has been taught that her reaction is not valid–in fact, her emotions seem to have upset her father.

Such a child may grow up gaslighting *herself*, invalidating her own feelings of sadness and putting on a mask of self-confidence. Because she believes that doubt and sadness about her appearance are unacceptable emotions, she never expresses these feelings to anyone else. Invalidation can have deep, deep roots!

If the father could set aside his own feelings about what he's hearing, he could more accurately appreciate what his daughter is going through and support her exactly where she is. He doesn't have to agree that she's ugly, or say she's right to feel bad about herself. All he has to do is acknowledge that she feels what she feels, and that's OK.

"Dad, the other girls at school keep saying I'm ugly."

"What?! Oh honey, I'm so sad to hear that. I can see how upset you are. Who wouldn't feel that way if someone said such a mean thing to them? Come sit here with me and tell me what happened."

Invalidation can certainly be intentional and manipulative, but more often than not it's unintentional and sometimes, plain clumsy. We might breezily say, "You've got this!" to someone who is desperately trying to tell us that they *don't*. Or we say, "Everything's going to be OK" to someone who feels like their whole world is falling apart. These things are intended to comfort, but they seldom do.

In fact, if a listener shows squeamishness about an emotion, their avoidance can send a deeply invalidating message: "The way you feel really *is* bad and scary. It's so bad and scary I don't even want to talk about it." If we show that we can't bear another person's emotional reality, how much harder must it feel for them to bear it?

Be mindful of accidental invalidation

Be aware of–and take ownership of–your own emotional reactions

Of course you're not a robot. You'll have your own feelings, your own opinions, and your own perceptions of what you hear. None of that needs to be hidden when you're listening empathetically to someone, but try to be aware that these reactions are in fact *yours*, and don't let defensiveness impair your ability to really listen. Set aside your own perspective and step fully into theirs.

Avoid making comparisons

We all try to make sense of the world by drawing connections and making associations, and it may seem natural to think of a way that the story you're hearing connects to something or someone else you know. But one way that invalidation can creep in is when we make comparisons. For example:

- We mention someone else who is also going through the same experience ("Oh yes, I know all about this. My friend has gone through *exactly* the same thing as you! You'll be fine.")

- We over-normalize ("Every single woman in the world goes through menopause, it's not a big deal.")
- We compare people against cultural standards, conventions, or even just fashion ("Most people love celebrating their birthdays, why don't you?")
- We might point out how others have it better or worse ("I know your leg hurts, but my uncle is an amputee, and he'd do anything just to have a leg!")

Comparisons can be invalidating because they imply that our emotions are somehow dependent on other peoples', which is simply not true. We feel how we feel! Focus on the emotions themselves, regardless of how they measure up to anything else.

Stay away from "should"

For the same reason, avoid language that suggests that there is a correct way to think or feel, whether you literally use the word "should" or not.

"You shouldn't get so worked up about this."

"Lighten up!"

"You should be a bit more grateful."

"What will other people think?"

When in doubt, don't

If you're ever feeling unsure, remember that instead of making a statement, you can always ask a thoughtful question instead. Remember that you can comfort and validate someone without having all the answers, and without having something useful to say. Just listen. If something doesn't make sense to you, ask an open-ended question.

"I'm sorry, there's something I'm just not getting. I *love* celebrating my birthday and I know others do too, but you say birthdays make you anxious. I'm really curious, what is it about them that stresses you out?"

Avoid giving unwanted advice

When was the last time you specifically asked someone for advice?

Can you recall the last time you thought to yourself, "I'd really like to hear someone's opinion on my personal troubles, and be told what they think I should do about them"?

While people do occasionally ask for advice, the truth is, it's a relatively rare occurrence! Simply consider when last you shared your feelings with someone just because you wanted to be heard, and you'll see that this is the stronger need by far. It seems like in the realm of advice, we really do agree with the maxim that "it's better to give than receive," with most of us greatly preferring to give guidance than to receive it!

Why are we so ready to step in and offer solutions? Let's take a closer look at a few hypothetical examples.

Example 1: A very overweight woman has been referred to a weight-loss clinic by her doctor. The woman expresses her embarrassment and anger to a friend, who happily empathizes and validates. The woman is advised by her friend that there's nothing wrong with her, that she should embrace her size, that the doctor (and the whole world, in fact) is fatphobic, and that she should report him for discrimination. The woman's friend is also overweight.

Example 2: A man opens up to a colleague about difficulties he is having parenting his son. The colleague listens intently, then sends him away with a dozen recommendations for books, podcasts, documentaries, and research papers. "I can't believe you haven't read Dr. So-and-So's work! You *have* to start there, he explains everything."

Example 3: A little child sees his mother crying one day. He thinks for a while and then offers her his half-eaten lollipop to make her feel better.

Example 4: You tell a close friend about the hellish morning you've had, and how your car broke down. They spend the next twenty minutes frantically trying to figure out what went wrong with the car, and how to prevent it happening again.

Now, each of these people has offered up advice, suggestions, and recommendations, but each of them has done so for slightly different reasons. People offer advice because:

- They are uncomfortable with the emotional content being shared, and find it awkward to be reminded about truths they themselves don't want to look at. The advice is given because it validates *them* and their choices.
- They want to demonstrate superior knowledge and wisdom, and relish the opportunity to show that they are in possession of the solution.
- They genuinely care about the other person and want to help them–but they can't quite imagine that what comforts them might not be comforting for someone else.
- They genuinely care and want to help, but have become distracted by the practical aspects of the "problem" and how to fix things, all while ignoring the emotional

reality. They may also just be excited to contribute and share what they know!

It's not that advice in itself is a bad idea; rather, it's that we tend to offer advice from within our own perspective, and so it becomes tainted with our needs and expectations. **This kind of advice centers us, instead of the person we're trying to help.** It is not that giving advice is wrong, and refraining from giving it is right. Rather, it comes down to validation. **Does our advice genuinely recognize and center that person's perspective? Is it really in *their* best interests?**

It can be incredibly difficult to offer up suggestions and opinions without a tiny amount of judgment creeping in. We casually tell people what to do to improve their health, how to spend their money, or what they should do in their relationships, without being cognizant of the ways this may make them feel invisible or unsupported.

Unsolicited advice can even veer into disrespect if it's based on unfounded or unkind presumptions. The offering up of comments and suggestions can feel intrusive, making it seem like the advice-giver really knows best, or that they're in the position to educate, correct, or enlighten the advice-receiver.

Advice of all kinds can be invalidating because it communicates a subtle message that a person is actually incapable of solving their own problems. Even worse, there can be the suggestion that that person's own judgment is not sufficient, and needs to be externally validated by others who, one way or another, know them better than they know themselves.

Something else to consider is that unsolicited advice often doesn't feel all that satisfying for the advice-giver, either! The advice is seldom taken or acted on, leaving them feel (ironically) un-listened to, and they may feel resentful, frustrated, or rejected. Soon, what began as a sincere desire to be helpful ends with a compulsion to control people, judge their choices, and interfere with their lives. It can impact our ability to empathize, too,

It's worth reiterating that **there is nothing wrong with advice in itself**. The world would be a strange place if human beings never tried to teach, guide, or even warn one another. What's important, perhaps, is the spirit behind the impulse to offer this advice. In our example earlier, we saw that the overweight woman was given advice by a doctor, who suggested she attend a particular clinic. If this was a competent doctor, they would have given this advice as a result of their medical training and expertise, as well as professional obligations to act in the best interests of the patient. In other words, the advice is (or should be) informed purely by what's best for the person receiving it.

This may be a fairly good yardstick against which to measure our own advice: **Will our recommendations genuinely help the person we're offering them to?** Or is the advice more about meeting our own needs?

Had she considered things from this perspective, the overweight woman's friend might have responded very differently. "Well, I certainly have my own views on the topic, and you'd never find *me* going to a weight-loss clinic in a million years... but if the doctor is recommending that you go, then I suppose that's something to take seriously. I care about you so my advice would be to do whatever's best for your health and wellbeing."

Understanding must precede intervention

In the absence of really knowing what is going on in someone's world, we tend to just project our own assumptions and opinions, and offer advice based off of that. Instead, seek first to understand and then–if you must–offer advice that is appropriate.

The single best way to gain more understanding is to be guided by compassionate curiosity, and ask open-ended questions, listening closely to the answers given. Here are a few useful tips for asking such questions:

Recognize your question's real intention

Be honest about what your question is really doing. Are you genuinely curious and wanting to understand, or does your question conceal a small desire to steer things, judge, or insert your own agenda?

Many people offer advice that is really just thinly veiled judgment, for example "Have you ever thought about going on antidepressants?" Instead, be honest if a less leading question may feel better for the one receiving it. "How are you feeling about things?"

Keep things open-ended

A closed question (that is, one that can be answered with a single word or a yes/no) is shutting down conversation, rather than opening it up. It's also a very sneaky way that judgment and assumption can creep in, and it may send the message that only one answer is right or desirable.

"Do you think maybe he's a narcissist?" (Introduces a topic, steers the conversation).

"Well do you want to say something, or don't you?" (Are there really only these two options? Says who?).

"Wouldn't you like to just move on from all this?" (Pushing someone to a conclusion).

Seek to understand, not fix

The urge to offer advice disappears if you can remind yourself of the thing that most people really want from you when they're opening up: emotional validation. That's all. When you understand that this is the value that you can offer them, you can focus on that and let go of everything else.

For similar reasons, avoid the temptation to assign blame or identify the bad guy, get to the root of the problem, or go on a fact-finding mission to find out "what really happened." None of that is really important. Remind yourself that in compassionate conversations, your main goal is to *first* perceive and validate emotions, then go from there.

Fighting toxic positivity

We cannot talk about unsolicited advice and emotionally invalidating responses without talking about toxic positivity. Even if you've never heard the term before, you doubtless recognize toxic positivity when you see it.

The darker side of greatly increased mental health awareness today, especially in social media, is a growing intolerance for "negativity" of any kind. **While positive thinking has obvious value, it can metastasize into its own insidious form of invalidation.**

The modern world is saturated with personal development ideology that assures us that happiness is a choice, and that our thoughts determine our reality. It follows then that if we are suffering, it's because our mindset isn't "right," we didn't have enlightened enough thoughts, our "vibe" was wrong, or we just plain didn't try hard enough. Either way, this is invalidation territory: our suffering is made unacceptable, shameful, invalid.

Add into this mix the influence of New Age thinking (particularly the "Law of Attraction") and you will be encouraged to conclude that you have "attracted" your own misfortune, manifested it through your own will, or even chosen it for yourself in a previous life.

On the surface, toxic positivity may look wholesome and positive, but beneath the inspirational quotes and affirmations may lie an unwillingness to accept, acknowledge, and validate negative emotions. **The fear is that acknowledging negative emotions**

somehow makes them more real or invites them into reality in unacceptable ways. So, toxic positivity is the attempt to avoid those genuine feelings of distress, downplay them, dismiss them, shame them, or explain them away.

Social media in particular offers reductive bite-size chunks that lack nuance and depth, and end up glossing over the genuine human experience, which includes *all* emotions, "good" and "bad." The impulse to dismiss or resist negativity is then turbocharged when it combines with certain oversimplified ideologies or philosophies.

For example, say you become seriously ill and start experiencing feelings of sadness and defeat:

- the Law of Attraction practitioner might say that it's because you "came into agreement" with some bad energies
- a Hindu may say it's Karma
- a TikTok influencer may blame your mindset
- a naturopath may tell you that your distress is because of trapped trauma or eating too much refined sugar
- a Christian may say not to worry because God works in mysterious ways

- a Buddhist may helpfully point out that the self is illusory anyway, and that suffering is just a result of your own desire and attachment.

Phew! Are any of these bite-size interpretations right? Maybe they are, and maybe they aren't. But take another look at each of them and you will find that what they all have in common is emotional invalidation. In their own ways, each dismisses and de-legitimizes suffering, perhaps implying that the sufferer has somehow invited or caused their own misery, or else that there's no point expressing or acknowledging it. By jumping in with a ready explanation that glosses over genuine distress, the speaker is essentially told that the way they really feel is unacceptable, illogical, unreasonable, unimportant, or even a little foolish.

In essence, toxic positivity is about encouraging a positive outlook even though it's not appropriate, and deliberately squashing awareness and expression of negative emotions. When paired with unwarranted advice from a place of superiority, it can be particularly devastating, making people feel crazy or stupid for feeling as they do. The "inspirational" quote comes across as subtle chastisement. Despite wanting to help, people can be cruelly impatient with other people's suffering, or frame their predicament in terms of a lack of enlightenment, strength, or effort.

The Psychology Group explains it this way,

> *"Toxic positivity is the excessive and ineffective overgeneralization of a happy, optimistic state across all situations. The process of toxic positivity results in the denial, minimization, and invalidation of the authentic human emotional experience.*
>
> *Just like anything done in excess, when positivity is used to cover up or silence the human experience, it becomes toxic. By disallowing the existence of certain feelings, we fall into a state of denial and repressed emotions. The truth is, humans are flawed. We get jealous, angry, resentful, and greedy. Sometimes life can just flat-out suck. By pretending that we are "positive vibes all day," we deny the validity of a genuine human experience."*

When positivity is used to invalidate real feelings, then it becomes toxic positivity. **The message behind toxic positivity is really simple: only positive feelings are acceptable. Negative ones aren't, (i.e. "good vibes only").** The sad result is relationships where people feel they have to wear masks and pretend if they want to be accepted. What a bad vibe!

What to say instead

Obviously, a pithy quote or inspiring anecdote can be a wonderful thing to share, and a welcome word of encouragement really can lift someone's spirits.

That said, here are some common toxic positivity clichés that you may want to try and rephrase.

Toxic positivity: "Count your blessings," "Think of everything you have to be grateful for," or even "In the midst of every crisis, lies great possibility."

The message it really sends: "You're not allowed to be unhappy."

What to say instead: "That sounds really hard. Tell me about it."

Toxic positivity: "Everything is energy," "Your thoughts create your reality," "Remember that positive attracts positive!"

The message it really sends: "You're to blame for being unhappy. You asked for it."

What to say instead: "Wow, how unlucky! I can't imagine how you must be feeling."

Toxic positivity: "Own your power," "Failure is not an option," "I know you can do it, be fierce!"

The message it really sends: "Weakness is unacceptable, and you should be ashamed if you feel that way."

What to say instead: "I know this must be hard. Can I do anything to support you?"

Toxic positivity: "That's just life," "Don't worry, be happy," "Ah well, it's not for us to understand," "Lao Tzu once said…"

The message it really sends: "Your suffering is irrelevant. I don't really want to think about it, and I wish you wouldn't either."

What to say instead: "I can tell something's really bothering you. Want to talk?"

Ultimately, most of us would prefer validation and recognition of the way we *really* feel, rather than be told what we *should* feel. Being truly heard is so much more validating than getting a lesson about looking on the bright side. The irony is that the quicker you are able to acknowledge someone's genuine experience, the quicker they can process and move on from it.

Self-disclosure

"When my business failed almost five years ago, I felt terrible, too. But you know what? It's not how many times you fall down. It's how many times you get up. Took me a long time to learn that one! Just get back up again, it's what I did. Would you believe that I was actually bankrupt back then? It was bad, we were living off of credit cards, we couldn't pay the mortgage. Much worse than what you're going through, believe me! But looking back now I can see that all along, I was teaching myself a lesson I needed to learn."

What do you make of this response to someone's expression of panic about their struggling business?

By this point, you can probably spot a few hallmarks of invalidation: the dismissive comparisons, the clichéd advice. But there is something else, too: a whole heap of self-disclosure. Very simply, **self-disclosure is when we offer revelations about our own personal lives, perhaps sharing memories, opinions, or things that have happened to us.**

In the previous few sections we saw that there is nothing inherently bad about offering advice, nor with sharing something positive and uplifting. The real trouble is *how*, *when*, and *why* we do these things. The same can be said about self-disclosure. Learning that someone you know has experienced the same thing as you can be reassuring. Self-disclosure can strengthen relationships, deepen intimacy, and inspire trust. When someone reveals a little of themselves, it can create a strong feeling of belonging and acceptance, and indirectly communicates support and validation.

Too little self-disclosure can be invalidating. It can make people feel like they alone are opening up and bearing the risk of being emotionally vulnerable, while we stand back, reluctant to reciprocate. Being a closed book in this way can rightly make people a little weary about sharing themselves. Remembering the Costly Signal Theory, we can see self-disclosure as a willingness to invest psychological resources into a relationship and make the effort. Self-disclosure is an honest signal because when we say, "I know how you feel," there is a genuine experience to back that up.

As you may have noticed from the opening example, however, self-disclosure is not automatically a validating move since it may inadvertently invite comparisons, judgments, assumptions, and all the rest. We need to find ways to self-disclose that are genuinely validating of the other person.

Striking the balance

How do we find the line between over-disclosing and being too aloof and impersonal? How can we share some of our experience without eclipsing theirs?

In the context of emotional validation, we can think of **appropriate self-disclosure as deliberate, minimal, and ultimately focused on the other person, not ourselves**. It's all about sharing in a strategic way. Does it increase trust, closeness, and connection? Does it help the other person feel seen and heard? Then it's likely to be appropriate. Another way to think about it is to **ask whether your disclosure helps and encourages the other person to express their feelings, or whether it interrupts, distorts, or hijacks that expression**.

Returning to our example, we could tweak the response to something like this:

"Well, I hear you. Some years back I had a little business trouble myself. Like you, we were terrified, and we weren't sure what we were going to do. But we got through it. If you ever need to vent or anything, I hope you know I'm here."

Keep it relevant

Share experiences that have a direct connection to what the other person is sharing. This can be a way of normalizing, since they'll realize that they are not alone.

Keep it brief

Anecdotes about your own life should be introduced as asides or tangents, i.e. they should not be shared in such a way that it feels like the conversation has permanently shifted away from the speaker. A sentence or two is enough.

Keep things balanced

Self-disclosure should match and mirror the emotional intensity of what the speaker is sharing with you. If they're talking about their dog that died, and you jump in with a story about the death of your grandparent, you may be responsible for a seriously awkward case of one-upmanship!

Keep a little distance

It's usually a good idea to share things that are firmly in the past, as current issues may be too raw and uncomfortable. In fact, if you share that you once struggled but can now look back on that struggle with calm acceptance, you quietly communicate reassurance and hope that they, too, will get through it.

Keep it pressure-free

Another reason to avoid current struggles is that the other person may feel an unspoken emotional demand from you, and feel that it's now *their* job to comfort and support *you*. Maintaining a tiny bit of distance and keeping your anecdote short will ensure that you are not suddenly making the interaction all about your own emotions.

Keep aware of timing

Try to choose a good moment to share a bit about yourself. An uncomfortable silence is usually *not* the right time, nor is it wise to interrupt a person as they're in the middle of a thought. Generally, self-disclosure is best placed at a distance from the most intense part of the conversation, and preferably not at the very beginning. In other words, make sure that you've spent some time genuinely listening and validating first, before sharing your experience.

Keep their values in mind

If you've been listening closely, you may have a good sense of what the speaker values, what their goals are, and their overall worldview. If you know this, then you can tailor your self-disclosure to reinforce and validate those values, rather than challenging or threatening them.

Keep it vague

Some of us play our cards close to our chests, and others are notorious over sharers. It's good to be aware of your own tendencies, and be mindful of *what* you're sharing, and *how much.*

Never share anything that is a literal secret (especially someone else's secret) or something that is likely to make you uncomfortable or regretful later on. When in doubt, share stories where the emotional content is highlighted, and be vague or general about the details. So, it's better to simply say that you too have experienced marital problems, rather than going into embarrassing, private details of exactly why.

Keep paying attention

Notice the effect your self-disclosure has and respond accordingly. The emotional energy shared in any discussion should feel broadly equal and reciprocal. If your disclosure is not met with much enthusiasm, or there's an uncomfortable response, try not to be offended or take it personally. Just dial things back a bit. While it's possible you may have misjudged, it's more likely that the other person is just not emotionally available to respond in any other way.

Before we conclude this section, we need to recognize the real risks of self-disclosure, and acknowledge the situations where it would be ill-advised. Avoid revealing yourself to people you know are untrustworthy, and be extremely cautious about sharing personal information in a professional context–even if you are invited to do so.

It's generally a bad idea to self-disclose at social events, or where alcohol is involved and people may be sharing far more than they really mean to. In the same way, be cautious about self-disclosure online or on social media, or revealing truly controversial details about yourself that could put you at risk.

Summary

- Invalidation is often accidental, but we can work to reword our responses to avoid careless or subtle dismissing, judging, blaming, or centering ourselves and our interpretations.
- Take ownership of your own emotional reactions, avoid making comparisons, and drop the word "should."

- When giving advice, ask yourself whether your input genuinely recognizes and centers that person's perspective, and whether it's in *their* best interests. Avoid advice that undermines someone's competence or judgment, and avoid making assumptions. Understanding must always precede intervention.
- While positive thinking has value, if used to deny or minimize genuine negative emotions, it can metastasize into invalidation. Toxic positivity is about encouraging a positive outlook even when not appropriate, and quashing awareness and expression of negative emotions.
- Self-disclosure is when we offer revelations about our own personal lives, memories, opinions, or things that have happened to us. Appropriate self-disclosure as deliberate, minimal, and focused on the other person, not ourselves. That way, we offer real emotional validation and help people feel less alone.

Chapter 5: Validation in the Face of Conflict

If you've made it this far into the book, your willingness to cultivate genuine empathy for others is clear–well done, that's something to be proud of! You may have resonated with some of the examples shared so far, and seen in them a glimpse of the relationships in your own life that you'd like to improve. And yet, perhaps at the back of your mind, you're also thinking about... someone else. This person may be someone that makes all your plans to be a more mindful communicator fly out the window: "Wait, do I also have to validate *them*?!"

In this chapter, we're ready to broach the slightly more complex topic of when to avoid validation, and how to navigate social situations where empathy and compassion need to be strategically applied, rather than taken as a default. The reason we've left this topic for last is because for most of us, our relational problems can only be helped by adding more compassion, more empathy, and more mindful listening. **If we're struggling to connect, emotional validation is really the best psychological "silver bullet" we have.**

Nevertheless, in this chapter, we'll consider all those times in life where we need to be a bit more deliberate in who we validate, when, and how. Namely, we'll look at times where the best approach is to step back, disengage, or even assert ourselves and our boundaries. We'll also look at how validation can be a powerful tool for diffusing conflict and friction–but only when used intelligently.

When is validation not the best approach?

No two human beings are the same. No two relationships are the same, either, nor are individual conversations within those relationships. We can try to identify certain patterns and rules of thumb, but at some point we need to use our own informed judgment about whether or not to validate someone's emotions. If you're feeling unsure about a particular dynamic or situation, consider whether it may be presenting one of the following red flags.

Validation red flags

Red flag 1: The person is causing harm to themselves or others, or may do so in future

We already know that when we validate, it is the person's feelings, worth, and perception that we are recognizing and accepting. It is not that we agree with or support their actions. Drawing this line, however, can be tricky, especially when someone's feelings and thoughts are directly connected to the harmful actions they're taking.

Be cautious about offering validation in situations where there is abuse, violence, addiction, or any dangerous or illegal activity, especially if a child or other vulnerable person is involved. While validation can go a long way to disarming people, calming immediate conflict, and helping people lower their defenses, when we continue to validate in the longer term, we become more complicit in the situation.

If a close friend confides in you about their abuse or deception towards their partner, for example, you may feel ethically conflicted. Validation here should focus on acknowledging your friend's responsibility and capacity to make the right decision–but without weighing in with advice that could quickly create complications. Depending on the circumstance, the wisest thing may be to step away completely, or to enlist the help of the proper authorities.

Red flag 2: Someone is stuck in the complaining pit

You already know what I mean by "complaining pit"! Someone who has become trapped in complaint has grown comfortable with their discomfort. You offer validation, and they repeat their grumble, you validate *that*, and they instantly find something else to moan about, and on and on.

When we're feeling bad, we might not be in the right frame of mind to think of solutions or ways out. But if someone is *consistently* unwilling to seek help, advice, or a solution to their problems, then your validation may actually be reinforcing their passivity. Essentially, you may become trapped in a kind of codependent relationship.

The way out is simple, if not always easy: offer validation along with a prompt to reconsider their own responsibility to deal with the things that make them unhappy. For example, you could say, "I hear how frustrated you are about this, and I can see that it's been bothering you for a while now. What do you think is something you can start doing about it?"

If someone persists, it's OK to set a gentle boundary. "Hey, I really understand how you're feeling, and I want to help, but I feel like we're covering the same ground over and over, and it's starting to drain me. Let's talk about something else." They won't like it, but setting a limit could finally spur them to action.

Red flag 3: They have asked you for advice, clarity, reassurance, or solutions

It's ironic, but sometimes what people find most validating is us responding to the facts of their situation, rather than their feelings. For example, if someone is setting a boundary with us, or making a request, we may wrongly go into recognizing and acknowledging their emotions, when all they want is for us to *do* something.

Likewise, if someone has deliberately asked for your opinion or advice, or they themselves are framing their predicament in terms of practical solutions, then your most validating move is to meet them where they are, and try to offer what they're asking for. Focusing on emotions when there's a real, external problem can feel frustrating and invalidating. If someone is distressed because, for example, they're finding something confusing or ambiguous, all that's needed from you may be to supply the necessary information, rather than repeatedly validate their feelings of confusion.

Red flag 4: You're dealing with unexamined emotions

Imagine Lina is angry at Chris for insulting her. Chris responds to this by validating Lina's angry emotion, saying, "I acknowledge that you're angry. You have every right to feel that way, and it makes sense that you do."

However, in this case, Lina's anger is actually based on a misinterpretation–namely, that she thought that Chris was insulting her with something he'd said earlier. The truth is he meant no harm and was not even talking to her. Lina's anger comes from her *interpretation* of his behavior, not his behavior. If he validates the anger, saying it makes sense, he is essentially saying that Lina's interpretation makes sense… when it doesn't. This may deepen and extend the misunderstanding, rather than clear it up. "So you *did* mean to insult me then?"

Validating feelings without having a real understanding of where they come from can be tricky, because it distorts the facts of the situation, and can create confusion. We may accidentally validate ideas and guesses that are causing disconnection. Validating emotions during disagreements is a good idea; however, it needs to be done after there is a full understanding of what has actually caused that disagreement.

Marriage therapist Dr. Catherine Aponte suggests that we don't validate so-called "unexamined emotions." Rather than automatically validating someone's "take" on reality, we can encourage self-reflection and understanding. How are people's thoughts, assumptions, and expectations coloring their perception? How is this creating their emotional reality?

There is no such thing as a free-standing emotion; all emotions are responses to our interpretation of events, and sometimes we are indeed mistaken in these interpretations. With more complex issues, a more fitting response is not to just blindly validate whatever emerges, but to carefully sort through the beliefs and appraisals that are leading to the emotion.

Red flag 5: We ourselves are not in the right mental space to offer validation

We're human, too. If we are tangled up in the same dynamic as the speaker, we may find ourselves trying to manage, express, and validate our own feelings. This can impact our ability to be fully present with them–and that's OK. Nobody is forced to play therapist to anyone else. We all have a right to our own boundaries, and to make our own needs a priority when necessary.

It can be tiring to listen to, understand, moderate, and "hold" other people's emotions–this is work in a very real sense. A little self-awareness will let you know when it's time to gracefully and tactfully step away (we will explore the necessity of *self-validation* at the very end of this chapter).

If you find yourself starting to feel a little resentful or undervalued, or that you're consistently incurring unacceptable costs in order to support others, remind yourself you don't have to be a martyr. Validation is a wonderful thing to offer people, but it's OK if you're not always the person to offer that validation.

Red flag 6: You're dealing with someone who feels helpless… but isn't

There is a difference between validating feelings and validating agency. A person may feel that they are stuck and hopeless and helpless, and we can validate that, but we need to be careful that we are not agreeing that they genuinely cannot act to help themselves.

According to licensed therapist TyaCamellia Stone of *Roots Relational Therapy*, we

> *"...need to move beyond validating emotions, and into validating a person's agency; their power to make change in their life [...] When people struggle with overwhelming negative emotion, they forget they have the power to make changes. Validating the negative feelings too much limits the client's self-perception of who they are and what they are capable of. [...] Emotional validation is important, but so is encouraging agency, courage, and resilience..."*

Offer validation, but be mindful of accidentally encouraging and supporting someone's victim mentality.

Red flag 7: They are experiencing mental illness or have a personality disorder

If you're feeling under the weather and a bit tired, keeping hydrated and having a good night's sleep is probably going to make you feel a lot better. However, if you've contracted a serious illness, you need proper medical intervention, and a night's sleep may help a little, but it certainly won't cure you!

Validation is like this–it's the "best medicine" for people dealing with the normal range of human experiences. Occasionally, however, validation is nowhere near enough, and we need to step aside and call in the professionals.

If someone is caught in serious depression or anxiety, your validation will absolutely be welcome and beneficial. It just may not be *enough*. Most psychotherapy makes liberal use of validation, normalization, and emotion labelling, and more acknowledgement and recognition of the reality of mental illness is never a bad thing. However, we need to recognize when someone's need may exceed our ability to help. We need to do what we can to help them receive more intensive support from mental health professionals.

Validation is necessary for people suffering from mental illness, but it alone is not sufficient. That said, there is one mental illness where validation is definitely contraindicated, and that's what we'll look at next.

Do not validate narcissistic people

Let's return then, to that earlier question–do we really have to validate *everyone*? For everything? The answer is, no!

Going back to basics, emotional validation is about meeting another person's all-too-human need to be seen, heard, and acknowledged as real and legitimate. This need often goes unmet, but when you *can* meet it, you create intimacy, trust, and closeness. Importantly, once met, that need then dissolves, and makes way for more relaxed, trusting, and respectful communication all round.

It follows then that we should not use validation when a person's need to be seen and heard is itself pathological. In other words, we need to avoid validation when it comes to narcissistic personalities. A person does not have to have diagnosed Narcissistic Personality Disorder to display exaggerated feelings of their own importance, and to unreasonably demand admiration, attention, and empathy. It's possible for all of us to engage in narcissistic behaviors now and then, without being narcissists.

Throughout this book we've made the claim that people are worthy of respect and acknowledgment, and that they deserve understanding and empathy. **When it comes to narcissism, however, we may be dealing with desires and "needs" that are not, in fact, valid.** When people are behaving narcissistically, they have no capacity to genuinely receive empathy nor reciprocate it.

Any attention and validation is likely to *increase* their demand for these things, not satisfy it. The more validation you show a person with this attitude, the more they'll gobble it up and expect more, all while the relationship suffers. Sooner or later, you'll start to feel abused. Ultimately, validation doesn't "work" on narcissistic people in the same way it does for others.

Taking things a little further, some people choose to deliberately abuse and take advantage of people's natural tendency to empathize, be vulnerable, and open up. In this case, validation is used against the one offering it, and twisted into a weapon. In such cases, it would be seriously dangerous to continue to validate, empathize, and connect.

Darlene Lancer, an expert on abusive relationships, writes in *Psychology Today* that,

> *"The most important thing to remember about intentional abuse is that it's designed to dominate you. Abusers' goals are to increase their control and authority, while creating doubt, shame, and dependency in their victims. They want to feel superior to avoid hidden feelings of inferiority."*

It would be a deadly mistake, then, to add to those feelings of superiority. Emotionally unhealthy people may gladly soak up any validation you offer and perceive it as evidence of their superiority, your agreement, or even your willingness to be dominated by them. A narcissist often cannot discern the difference between validation and agreement, and some may even quietly conclude that your kindness and consideration is proof that they are better than you!

If a person is operating in the realm of anxious control, grandiose superiority, and a need to constantly assert dominance, then any sincerity you offer will be twisted, and used to fuel yet more narcissism. For healthy people, validation is an invitation to more genuine human connection. For narcissists, validation is something only weak people offer to others in recognition of their superiority. In other words, they can only see your compassion as an opportunity for them to exploit you.

Instead of giving and giving and giving, **we need to draw and assert firm boundaries**. We must understand that we should not persist in "helping" others if it begins to harm us. Now, none of this is to say that narcissists are monsters who deserve harsh treatment, or that people can't change. But it is worth being crystal clear about when you should be (or indeed can be) responsible for making that change. You can certainly offer a narcissist politeness, respect, and consideration–but do so while remaining mindful of your boundaries.

Signs you are dealing with a narcissist

We are told that we live in an era of narcissism, so much so that accusing people of being narcissists has become a popular everyday hobby! Jokes aside, the tips already described will help you guard against other people's narcissistic *behavior*, but what about those real narcissists out there, the people who permanently lack empathy and are genuinely convinced of their special importance?

The Diagnostic and Statistical Manual tells us that a person may have NPD if they meet at least 5 of the following criteria:

- A grandiose sense of self-importance, such as exaggerating achievements and talents, expecting to be recognized as superior even without commensurate achievements

- Preoccupation with fantasies of success, power, beauty, and idealization

- Belief in being "special" and that they can only be understood by or associated with other high-status people (or institutions)

- Demanding excessive admiration
- Sense of entitlement
- Exploitative behaviors
- Lack of empathy
- Envy towards others or beliefs that others are envious of them
- Arrogant, haughty behaviors and attitudes

Those with genuine NPD may be boastful, attention-seeking, and have poor impulse control. They often have little insight into their own behavior, and do not believe that there is anything wrong with them. They may be both unwilling and unable to show vulnerability, to admit mistakes, or to validate other people. Their sense of superiority can be so enormous it can border on delusional.

If you find yourself dealing with someone who shows 5 or more of these traits, be careful. If a person demonstrates *some* of these traits, it may be more appropriate to say that while they're acting selfishly or have a big ego, they are not narcissists in the *clinical* sense. Nevertheless, narcissism to any degree requires extra caution.

Be clear on your boundaries

Know your own limits and stick to them. Pay close attention to your own energy levels, and the dynamics in your conversations with this person. If their demand for attention or validation starts becoming excessive, don't feel guilty about removing yourself from the situation. "I understand what you're saying, but I need to focus on other things right now." Be polite, be firm, and don't feel the need to explain or justify yourself.

If you're dealing with someone who is temporarily behaving in a selfish or inconsiderate way, you can say, "I really appreciate how you're feeling, but I need to take care of myself, too. Let's shelve this for now. We can talk about it later and see if we can have a conversation that respects the needs of both of us."

Validation during disagreements

A proper consideration for how to resolve deep conflict and work through serious relational issues is beyond the scope of this book. Nevertheless, while validation cannot fix all problems overnight, it can be an enormous help in preventing minor disagreements from turning into major ones. Everyday frictions and misunderstandings frequently come down to poor alignment in expectations, communication style, and plain old lack of empathy.

According to John Gray, the author of the now well-known *Men Are from Mars and Women Are from Venus*, **human beings differ in the ways that they give and receive validation. One particularly stable point of difference is gender, i.e. men and women tend to have different approaches to communicating**, which may cause avoidable arguments. Even if the stereotypical traits do not map neatly onto the male/female binary, you may discover that people do seem to differ in their personalities and perspectives, whether they're men or women.

Having a fuller understanding of these differences means we're better equipped to acknowledge and defuse them when they pop up. It's not an exaggeration to say that in some arguments, only 10% of the conflict is due to a genuine problem, with the remainder coming down to interpretation, reaction, and assumption... that is, it comes from the way people communicate *about* that problem.

Men versus women

Men and women differ in their communication styles. Bearing in mind that there are always exceptions, Gray points out that women tend to assume that their emotions are more obvious to men than they really are. This means that instead of communicating their emotions clearly and directly, they express them indirectly, often with the unconscious assumption that the listener will just automatically know what is happening, and what is required of them.

So, for example, a woman may feel disappointed, but instead of saying, "You said you were taking us out this evening. I'm really disappointed that you forgot," she may say, "How could you be so inconsiderate?" This is then (rightly) felt to be an attack by the man.

On the man's side, his primary need is for approval and recognition. According to Dr. Gray, a woman's disapproval is especially painful to a man, and if a woman is communicating in a way that feels to a man like disapproval, then an argument is not far off, as he will feel compelled to defend himself. Can you detect the underlying theme of validation in both their positions?

Of course, men also bear some of the responsibility for such misunderstandings. They tend to communicate in ways that focus on facts and details, rather than emotions. This of course amounts to emotional invalidation, even if that's not what is intended.

In our example, the woman telling him, "How could you be so inconsiderate?" triggers his defensiveness. But his own communication style means he may be unable to hear the hidden emotional content of what the woman is saying, and her indirect bid for validation. In response he focuses on logical explanations and justifications that protect his own ego. "Well, can you blame me for forgetting? I had a thousand things to remember at work today, and besides, the place you wanted to go to is closed today."

As you can see, misunderstanding and invalidation only cause… more misunderstanding and invalidation. The woman may hear all these "logical explanations" and perceive them as mere excuses, designed to imply that her disappointment is not warranted, that his work is more important than hers, or that she is being too difficult or needy. The more they argue, the more disconnected she feels, and the more judged and condemned he feels. Things may worsen even further from there.

So what's the way out? How can we use emotional validation to correct occasional mismatches and frictions between different communication styles? The trick is to maintain a spirit of respect and awareness of the other person's emotions even when we're in the midst of a tense discussion, and even when we're feeling plenty of emotion ourselves.

Tip 1: Really hear them out

Both men and women can launch into defensiveness before they've let the other one fully express themselves. Instead, slow down and let them speak. There is no rush. Allow them to express their point to completion, no matter how ridiculous that point may seem to you.

Stop yourself jumping in with interruptions or counterarguments, but also refrain from responding to them in your mind as they speak, when you should be listening. Letting people talk not only gives you the space to fully hear their perspective, but it softens their defenses and makes them more willing to listen to you when it's your time to talk.

Tip 2: Ask questions

Behind the accusation "How could you be so inconsiderate?" is a genuine lack of understanding: "I don't know what happened, or what it means." To gain a better understanding of the situation before reacting to it, we can make efforts to ask questions.

"Did you forget?"

"It's unlike you to forget things, what happened?"

"It seems like we agreed to this together. Have I got that right?"

Tip 3: Instead of "but," say "and"

The idea here is to introduce your own perspective without framing it as a contrast or threat to theirs. Using "and" also makes sure we aren't cancelling out any validation we've already offered.

For example, "I know you're stressed out and you didn't mean it, *but*..."

Instead of framing things this way, keep your communication constructive and cooperative. "I realize you're stressed out at work, *and* I've been feeling a bit lonely and was looking forward to spending time with you."

Tip 4: Offer a validation sandwich

Listen, validate the emotions you hear, then offer your own perspective, before offering more validation. This way you are asserting yourself, but at the same time disarming any defensiveness. This technique allows them to feel heard and respected, and you're still able to give your own perspective.

In our example, the man could say, "OK, I can see that this has really upset you, and that you're feeling disappointed in me. It makes sense that you'd feel that way. I've been pretty busy and distracted with work, and from my perspective, it was never my intention to hurt you. I can see that all you wanted was to spend time together. You were right to share your feelings with me, thank you for speaking up. I'm glad we talked."

We are all different

Though Dr. Gray's 1998 manual may strike some today as a little reductive or outdated, the real value comes from understanding that **people have different emotional needs, expectations, and behaviors. If we want our relationships to thrive, we need to recognize and validate people despite these differences**, rather than going to war with the differences themselves.

If we learn to consistently have empathy for the emotions beneath our differences, then we maintain connection. A few universal pointers for both men and women:

- People have different communication styles. Men tend to value approval and appreciation, while woman value being loved and cared for.
- Women tend to share problems in order to receive emotional validation, not to receive solutions or advice.
- Both men and women have emotional needs that they crave validation for, regardless of how they communicate those needs.

- Men tend to be more solutions-focused and practical, while woman are more empathetic and understanding–but when talking to someone of the opposite sex, have deep empathy and try to speak to *their* perspective, rather than insisting on your own.
- Man or woman, every person is an individual. We all have a unique way of communicating, and none of us does it perfectly. To minimize disagreements, remember to not only validate people's emotions and what they're saying, but the validity of their entire frame of reference, even if it's different from yours.

Don't gaslight!

Along with "trigger" and "narcissist," the term "gaslighting" may be on the list of most overused psychology terms in the public consciousness today. Originally inspired by the 1944 movie *Gaslight* (a recommended watch), this term is now applied to a wide range of quite different behaviors.

For clarity, let's first consider a working definition: **to gaslight someone is to manipulate them into questioning their own sanity, memory, and judgment.** Gaslighting is invalidation, but it's slightly different to the emotional invalidation already explored. In a way gaslighting goes further–it constitutes **a deliberate attempt to invalidate someone's entire reality and their grounding within that reality**. "Crazy making" comes to mind.

For extra clarity, let's also be clear what gaslighting *isn't*: it's not disagreement, and it's not merely disliking what someone is saying. Someone having a strong opinion, a different memory of events, a different view of things, or a desire to defend themselves ("that's not what I said!") is not gaslighting.

While nobody likes to be gaslit, our focus in this chapter is to be honest about our own tendency to gaslight others, whether intentionally or unintentionally. As an expression of manipulative control and abuse, gaslighting can be seen as a *deliberate* attempt to distort someone's sense of sanity, so as to better control them. While this is extremely serious, we will not be focusing on this type of abuse, but rather the more subtle and invisible forms of gaslighting that we can fall into without thinking.

Gaslighting is a potent form of invalidation

When we invalidate someone's perception of reality and their judgment, we are manipulating via distortion. The purpose of such behavior is to increase our own sense of power and control, and ironically, **to meet our own needs for validation**. Unfortunately, the cost is that we make other people feel less valid, i.e. crazy, mistaken, or mentally unstable. If you believe you would never do such a cruel thing, think again! Low-level gaslighting is more common than you think.

Gaslighting behavior 1: You make people with different opinions feel wrong

- Do you frequently try to educate, correct, or enlighten people?
- Do you subtly "punish" people for having different opinions?
- Are others afraid to disagree with you, or do they find it hard to respond to you?

People have different opinions. It's only natural. Sometimes we may strongly disagree with someone, and that's natural, too. We gaslight them, however, when we make them feel that they are not different, but actually *wrong*.

This reflects an attitude that on a fundamental level, people don't have a right to their views, and that their difference is actually a mistake of perception. We can disagree with someone without entirely discrediting their right to form their own views.

Gaslighting behavior 2: You tell "white lies"

- Do you sometimes deliberately "twist" the facts a little to get your own way?
- Do you fail to correct misunderstandings if they're in your favor?
- Do you conceal information in order to get approval or consent that you otherwise wouldn't get?

Sometimes a little tact and diplomacy is needed. It counts as gaslighting, however, when we tell small lies in order to conceal our mistakes, make ourselves look better, or gently push situations in our favor. If you've ever claimed to "forget" that you said someone something when you really didn't, or claimed that someone didn't say something when you know they did, then this is gaslighting because you are distorting and denying the other person's honest recollections.

Gaslighting behavior: You constantly instill doubt

- Have you ever said, "I'd like to hear the other side of the story." to someone expressing their hurt?
- Have you ever insinuated that someone's perception is down to a poor memory, a vivid imagination, or a lack of legitimate understanding?

- Have you ever positioned yourself as an expert who knows or can determine "what really happened" while casting doubt over someone's ability to do the same?
- Have you ever responded to someone's expression of emotion and then *corrected* them, telling them that they don't in fact feel that way?

If we regularly downplay people's emotions and reactions, and we insist on forcing our own judgment as a kind of superior way of making sense of the situation, we are in fact disempowering and undermining that person. A common example is to suggest that someone is just "making something up" or has merely misremembered something. Why should *your* memory be accurate but *theirs* is faulty? **The implication is that you are valid, and they are not.**

Similarly, when we make out as though someone is overreacting, or has misunderstood a situation, we are not only saying that their ability to perceive and make sense of the world is faulty, but also that our ability is superior to theirs–which is where the control comes in. Second-guessing people's expressions of their experience, instilling doubt about the veracity of their claims, and discrediting their appraisals can make them feel that there is something seriously wrong with them, that they are crazy, silly, or otherwise unintelligent.

You don't need to be told that **gaslighting is incredibly damaging behavior that can actually *cause* feelings of confusion and disorientation**. Over time, the distortions of the gaslighter can become internalized, and their victims learn to invalidate themselves, eventually doubting their own sanity.

But even the "milder" forms of gaslighting can be devastating. It's no exaggeration to say that our world is built on the assumption that some people have more of a right to define and assert their reality than do others. Valid eyewitness testimony may be discounted because it comes from someone we don't wish to grant that privilege; doctors validate the pain of some patients while claiming that the pain of other patients is "all in their heads"; politicians refuse to acknowledge their opponents' differences, insisting that they are *literally insane* to hold the opinions they do, and so on and so on.

Though this sounds like truly toxic behavior, the truth is that **many of us can fall into the trap of thinking that there is something inherently more valid about our own**

perceptions and judgments, simply because they're our own.

If you recognize any of this behavior in yourself, that's a good thing–awareness is the first step. Rather than making excuses (which is yet more gaslighting!) commit to recognizing your behavior and making genuine change. Behind most gaslighting behavior is a lack of empathy, a desire to control, and a sincere attempt to meet our own valid needs, albeit in unhealthy ways.

In keeping with a recurrent theme of this book, be extra-careful about gaslighting people precisely because you want to help and support them. For example, if someone tells you that they're feeling fearful, and you say, "Are you afraid, or are you just excited to be going outside your comfort zone?" you have actually introduced a tiny grain of doubt, and undermined their own self-perception.

Similarly, because you genuinely want to be helpful, you say something like, "I can see you're upset right now, and that's probably why things look so exaggerated to you. You'll change your mind in the morning once you've calmed down." Again, in the face of empathetic affect labelling, we can sneak in invalidation, making the claim that our take on the situation is somehow more legitimate than theirs.

Drop the distortion

Avoid gaslighting phrases and expressions, such as:

- "Are you sure? Did that really happen? Really? *Really?*"
- "You're imagining things."
- "Maybe you dreamt it."
- "That's not what happened."
- "Are you OK? Maybe you need professional help or something."
- "You're being paranoid."
- "I'm sure it seems that way to *you*" (implication: it isn't that way in reality).
- "What's wrong with you?"
- "*Actually*, what happened was…"
- "Were you drunk / hormonal / half asleep / off your meds?"
- "You only think that because you're a XYZ" (implication: your view is not an accurate reflection of reality, but a distortion attributable solely to your identity).
- "I was just joking" or "I was only trying to help."
- "That's crazy."

Finally, one extra deceptive thing to do is to suggest that other people are gaslighting *you*– in order to better control them. It goes without saying that using the language of abuse and victimhood to abuse and victimize someone else is extremely toxic behavior!

Try to remind yourself that no matter what, **other people's perspectives are as valid as your own**, and that it's not for us to judge who deserves the right to validity, and who doesn't. Respect perceptual boundaries, which means respecting that we all have a right to our own perceptions–but we do not have a right to *other people's* perceptions.

Finally, recognize that conflict is normal. We can resolve those conflicts, meet our needs, and find greater connection without ever resorting to manipulative control of the other person's mind.

The responsibility to self-validate

We've now reached an interesting point in our journey towards greater emotional validation of others, namely, the recognition of our own obligation to validate ourselves. As you might have noticed, so much invalidating behavior stems from an unhealthy attempt to have our own needs met, to express ourselves, and to control the way people respond to us. It follows then that **one of the best things we can do to become better communicators is learn how to meet and validate our needs in a healthy way**, so that we are not tempted to do so via the invalidation of others.

During emotionally difficult conversations, arguments, or conflicts, it can sometimes feel challenging to find the line between our needs and theirs, our perceptions and theirs. Occasionally, it can even feel like worth and value themselves are contested, and the conversation is a subtle tug-of-war to decide who is "right" and who gets to be the valid one.

Our book has focused on ways to use empathy, understanding, and real listening to correct this tendency. Approaching this problem from the other side, however, means becoming more aware of ourselves, our needs, and our boundaries.

Knowing how to self-validate will keep you from invalidating others, but it will also protect you from the invalidation of others. Psychologically speaking, we are talking about developing the ability to "stay in your lane"! If we understand that the emotional invalidation of others so often stems from our own feelings of not being validated, then we can understand the importance of learning to own our own feelings, to ask respectfully for what we need, and to find worth within, rather than constantly seeking it from others (or forcing it!).

All the things we have spoken about offering to others–recognition, acknowledgment of emotions, listening, attention, respect, understanding, consideration–are things that we have a duty to offer ourselves, too. Of course it is human nature to crave all these things from others. At the same time, emotional wellbeing also rests on the ability to have faith in our own value and validity, regardless of what others say or do.

It may seem counterintuitive, but **people who struggle to validate others tend to struggle to validate themselves**. If we fail to recognize our own value, how could we recognize it in others? To determine if you may have trouble self-validating, see how many of the following statements you agree with:

- I know my needs and limits
- I can comfortably express those needs and limits with my boundaries
- I know that I have innate worth as a human being
- I can encourage myself
- I know my strengths and am able to recognize my efforts, success, and progress
- I know how to be kind to myself

- I can accept my flaws and weaknesses, and acknowledge when I've made a mistake

- I am comfortable validating others

If you found it hard to say "yes" to the above, or else you know you have a problem with self-criticism, self-judgment or a habit of downplaying your needs, perceptions and limits, then you may need to work a little harder on self-validation.

External validation comes from other people–namely their recognition and acknowledgement of us. People can validate us by listening to us, reflecting our experience, accepting and respecting us, and recognizing our innate value.

Internal validation comes from within us–namely we recognize and acknowledge ourselves. We validate ourselves when we reflect internally, accept and respect our experience, and recognize our own innate value.

Sometimes, when two people who are overly dependent on external validation encounter one another, the conversation can devolve into manipulative behavior, as both parties attempt to extract for themselves the kind of recognition and acknowledgment that they are ironically unable to grant the other!

How to cultivate internal validation

Validating yourself does **not** mean becoming a narcissist, becoming self-aggrandizing, or elevating yourself above others. Rather, it's a healthy and mature way to claim your own worth, accept your experience, and find contentment from within (Martin, 2019. *Why It's So Important to Validate Yourself and How to Start*). The goal is not to flatter yourself into thinking that you're perfect, but rather to have the willingness to acknowledge your own imperfection with kindness and respect.

Knowing how to self-validate will make you more relaxed, resilient, and confident. It prepares you to accept both praise and criticism in a balanced, healthy way, and promotes genuine, authentic interaction with others. You're better able to find compassion for yourself, as well as for others, which means relationships of all kinds become deeper and more harmonious.

Here are a few ways to slowly develop a self-validating attitude:

Be mindful and just notice

Pay attention to how you're feeling. This opens the door to more autonomy and emotional self-regulation. "Hm, I'm feeling a little grumpy all of a sudden. I think I need a break."

Acknowledge your emotion without judging it

Practice affect labelling without attaching value judgments. "I noticed I felt strongly jealous back there" is sufficient; you don't need to condemn yourself for feeling jealousy. "It's OK that I feel jealousy. It makes sense to respond this way when I'm feeling insecure."

Remind yourself that emotions don't define you

We don't need to over-identify with feelings. No single experience defines us as people. Say, "I'm feeling jealous right now" rather than "I'm a jealous person." All emotions are temporary.

Offer yourself validating statements

They work when offered to other people, and they work when we offer them to ourselves!

- Having emotions is normal
- My feelings are valid
- It's OK to struggle sometimes. What do I need to feel better?
- I don't have to have it all figured out
- I'm doing my best
- I'm a human being worthy of understanding, compassion and respect

- I am so much more than my achievements or failures
- My value isn't dependent on other people's opinions
- Everyone makes mistakes/nobody's perfect
- It's OK to listen to my intuition
- I don't have to be liked by everyone
- I like myself
- I trust my judgment
- I have both good and bad traits, and that's OK

Treat yourself like you would a best friend

Some of us engage in self-talk that, if applied to anyone else, would constitute verbal abuse! If you're finding it hard to give yourself compassion, turn things around and imagine how you'd speak to a dear friend, or imagine how that dear friend would speak to you. Be nice to yourself.

Remember that you can give yourself what others haven't given you

So much unhealthy behavior comes from our misguided attempts to extract validation from others. But the truth is that we also possess the ability to grant that validation to ourselves. Think about the last time you felt invalidated by someone, and see if you can give yourself recognition you needed in that moment.

We don't give ourselves kindness and understanding because we deserve it, or because we are somehow better than others. We give it simply because we are human beings, we have value and dignity, and we are doing our best. It's OK to be flawed and to struggle sometimes–that doesn't make us any less worthy of understanding and sympathy. We take care of ourselves because we value the relationship we have with ourselves, and we take care of others because we value the relationships we have with them–regardless of our respective flaws and blind spots.

Once we can truly grasp this principle, compassion in both directions flows more easily. Instead of getting trapped in conflicts where both are desperate to force the other to see and hear us, we can **rest in our own value**, and encounter one another with more maturity, authenticity, curiosity, and joy.

Summary

- While emotional validation is the closest thing we have to a psychological silver bullet, it's not always the best approach. We need to be mindful and strategic in certain circumstances, for example in

- instances of abuse, mental illness, or when a person is chronic complainer.
- We should definitely not validate narcissists, i.e. when a person's need to be seen and heard is itself pathological. We can offer narcissists politeness, respect, and consideration, but in a mindful, boundaried way.
- Validation can help stop minor disagreements turning into major ones. People differ in their communication styles, especially men compared with women. Some people may have greater need for love and cherishing, while others value recognition and approval. It's worth meeting people where they are with empathy and curiosity.
- People have different emotional needs, expectations, and behaviors. We need to recognize and validate people despite these differences.
- Gaslighting is deliberately manipulating someone into questioning their own sanity, memory, and judgment, but we can also unintentionally gaslight people. Try not to instill doubt, label people's opinions wrong, tell white lies, or dismiss their perspective as inferior in any way. Conflict is normal but can be resolved without gaslighting.

- Finally, one way to become a better communicator is learn to meet and validate our needs in a healthy way, i.e. practice self-validation.

The art of compassion can take a lifetime to master. However, if we can cultivate a genuine appreciation for how truly fascinating people really are, and how much of a privilege it is to get to connect with them, then we may discover that we don't mind!

The insight is that we lose nothing by validating, respecting, and listening to others. In fact, the opposite is true. The more attentive listening and empathy we give, the more of it we seem to have, and the more we strive to understand others as they understand themselves, the more sense our own world seems to make to us.

We've covered empathetic listening and validation from many different angles in this book, but the hope is that as you go forth and practice these skills and principles in the laboratory of your own life, you find unique and creative ways to make them your own. And at the end of the day, if you're ever unsure of how to approach a particular person or situation, or you find it difficult to see where they're coming from, remember that you always have access to the ultimate resource: *them!*

Be willing to be surprised. Open yourself up to being taught, and you can learn anything–and arguably there is no subject more worth your while than the sincere understanding of the hearts and minds of others.

www.ingramcontent.com/pod-product-compliance
Lightning Source LLC
Chambersburg PA
CBHW060606080526
44585CB00013B/699